Blairsville Joint
Junior High School

92-Biog
Gan

DATE DUE

634

DL 100		
OCT 16		
OCT 28		
MAR 25		
NOV 14		
MAY 15		
MAR 23 '84		
APR 8 '84		
OCT 8		
OCT 9		
OCT 22 1997		
AP 06 '01		
AP 21 '05		

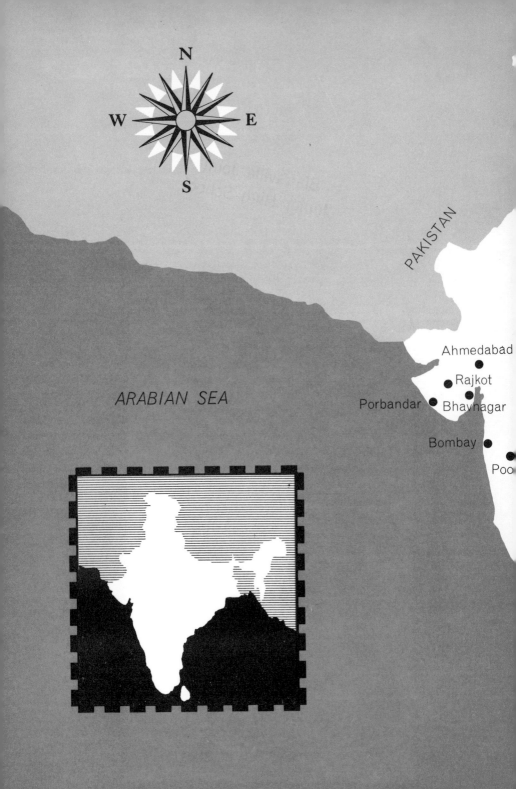

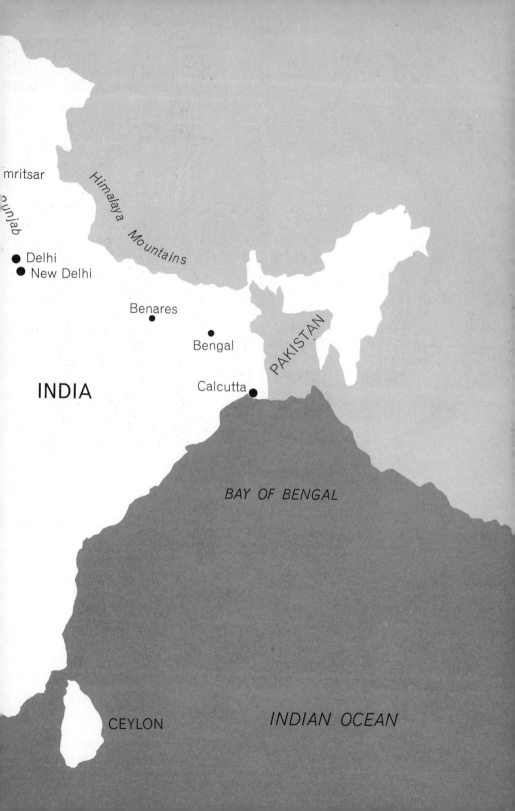

the true story of

GANDHI

MAN OF PEACE

BY REGINALD REYNOLDS

CHILDRENS PRESS, CHICAGO

92-Biog
Gan

American edition published through the courtesy of
Frederick Muller Limited
London

Library of Congress Catalog Card Number: 64-12907
Copyright © in Great Britain, 1959, Reginald Reynolds
© 1964, Childrens Press
Lithographed in the U.S.A.

Contents

Foreword

Author and Artist 10

The Boy Mohandas 13

Bewildered Student in London 27

Timid, Tongue-Tied Lawyer 41

The Struggle for Dignity 55

Quiet, Dignified Resistance 69

A New Kind of Leader 89

Rising Tide of Patriotism 97

Fight Without Violence 109

From Palace to Prison 123

The Price of Victory 129

Index of Place Names 140

Credits 141

Foreword

Gandhi was not very clever as a child. He was easily frightened. As a young man he was a failure in his first efforts as a lawyer. Then, suddenly, things began to happen.

A leader of men came into being, a man of great courage with a new way of looking at old problems.

Here is Gandhi's story—his boyhood in India; his student days in England; his experiences in South Africa through which he found his own way of fighting for truth and justice; his leadership of his own people in India in a struggle that ended in their victory and his death.

Gandhi won the respect of the world. Indeed, he was loved by millions who had never seen him.

Author and Artist

Reginald Reynolds was a member of a prominent Quaker family in London. He traveled widely and knew and worked with Gandhi in India. Mr. Reynolds died in Japan a few years ago. His widow is the well-known English author Ethel Mannin.

Parviz Sadighian was born in Tehran, Iran, in 1939. He was graduated from the Academy of Fine Arts in Tehran and received a partial scholarship for foreign study. In 1959 he enrolled at the Art Institute in Chicago and continued his studies in sculpture and in painting. Interest in painting led to courses in illustration and advertising art. Mr. Sadighian is now associated with the Bert Ray Studio in Chicago.

the true story of

GANDHI

The Boy Mohandas

If you like sailing ships and old seaports you would probably enjoy Porbandar. Brown-skinned fishermen clamber barefoot in the curious rigging of boats such as Sinbad the Sailor might have sailed.

Porbandar is an old port with its own history of trade with Africa through waters once infested with pirates, and the boy who grew up there must have heard many strange stories of Africa and the sea.

The town was once the capital of a small state, ruled by an Indian Prince. The Prince was not really independent. Hundreds of miles away a British Viceroy ruled over the whole of India, and the Viceroy was himself the servant of the British King or Queen. It was in 1869, in the reign of Queen Victoria, that a boy called Mohandas was born at Porbandar.

The boy's father was Kaba Gandhi, *Diwan* (or Prime Minister) of the little state. Kaba Gandhi lived in quite a small house, with a little window overlooking a small courtyard. Sitting at this window, Kaba Gandhi could listen to complaints and petitions from the subjects of the Prince, as kings and their ministers did in ancient times. Porbandar State was so small that the *Diwan* probably knew many of the people who came to ask for justice or for mercy.

Kaba Gandhi was himself a simple man who probably understood the troubles of other simple people. "He had no education, save that of experience," Mohandas said, many years later. "He was truthful, brave and generous, but short tempered."

Mohandas always remembered his mother as a true saint. The family were Hindus—people who practiced the ancient religion of India. The practice of Hinduism includes regular prayers and frequent fasts for those who take it seriously. Once Mohandas knew that his mother had vowed not to have any food unless the sun was shining. Little Mohandas and the other children watched for the sun to appear, for it was the rainy season, a time of dark clouds and heavy storms.

14

Mohandas was too young to understand why his mother made these strange vows. He only knew that she kept them bravely, going on with her usual work and never complaining. He also knew that she was much respected as a person of good sense. These were among the early memories which Mohandas took with him when the family moved to the state of Rajkot. Of his first school at Porbandar the boy remembered nothing except the names which the boys invented for the school master and the difficulty he had with the multiplication tables.

The Gandhi family left Porbandar when Mohandas was seven years old. His father had accepted the offer of a similar position at Rajkot, another of the small states in Kathiawar. If you look at a map of India you will see that there is a peninsula jutting out on the west coast, to the north of the great city of Bombay. The peninsula was called Kathiawar in those days, but if your map is a new one it will be called Saurashtra. And there you will see the port of Porbandar, the "White City," and Rajkot lying inland. The peninsula does not look very large in a map of India, but there are about as many people living there as you will find in the whole of Denmark, and you can make a nine-hour train journey through what was once the network of small Kathiawar states, each with its own *raja,* or prince.

Mohandas was a strange boy. He was shy of talking to people and always afraid that people would laugh at him. But perhaps the outstanding thing in him was gentleness. India is a country where there has often been fierce fighting

15

between people of different religions, like the fighting between Catholics and Protestants in England and Ireland and many parts of Europe, which was once so frequent and so bitter. But in the Gandhi home men of other religions would come to see the *Diwan* on official business. They were courteously received and often stayed long, talking of their own beliefs and traditions. So, from the beginning, the boy grew up to respect people of other religions. He could not see why people should wish to fight because they did not agree about everything. Following the example of his father and mother, who were just and generous and died quite poor for people in their position, Mohandas was never attracted to the idea of making large sums of money. "Truth," he tells us, "became my sole objective." That did not mean merely speaking truth but trying to know the truth about things the best way of all, which is the way of experiment.

Even in India, where life is very different in so many ways, Mohandas must have seemed odd to other people; but when he was thirteen something happened which had nothing to do with the peculiar character of Mohandas but a lot to do with the old customs of India. The shy schoolboy was married.

In those days it was usual for Indians to marry even younger than that. The marriage would be arranged by the parents on both sides. Mohandas married a girl of about his own age, called Kasturbai, who came from his old home town, Porbandar. Hindus always married members of the same "caste," so that if your father belonged to the caste

16

of priests you married someone of that caste, and the same would apply to people of the warrior caste. Kasturbai's family, like the Gandhis, were *Banias*. The *Banias* are all supposed to be merchants, and Kasturbai's father was one— a wealthy merchant, too—though the Gandhi family had given up trade when Kaba's grandfather began a new career for his sons and grandsons by entering the service of a prince.

They say that Kasturbai was a beautiful child. She was provided with the finest clothes and jewelry by her wealthy father, fitting to such an important occasion, for was she not to marry the youngest son of a Prime Minister? It was indeed a high honor for the girl and her family. Great preparations were made at the "White City" for the wedding. There was to be feasting and music, with no sparing of expense.

In those days there was no railway to Porbandar. The journey had to be made over rough roads; and by bullock wagon (the usual method of transport) this meant a five-day journey. At the last moment the Raja of Rajkot, to the dismay of the Gandhi family, said that he required his *Diwan* at the Court, on urgent business. Perhaps he was only playing with poor Kaba Gandhi, enjoying the exercise of power, like a Sultan or Caliph in the Arabian Nights, waiting for the moment when he could spring his wonderful surprise on the worried family. For he knew as well as anyone how important a wedding was and what a disgrace threatened his wretched Prime Minister. Suddenly he gave way. Was it too late? Not at all—special stagecoaches should be used! They would soon pass the lumbering bullock carts and his *Diwan* would arrive in great style, suitable for the highest minister of the Raja to Rajkot.

Perhaps they hurried too much over the bumps and potholes. Kaba Gandhi did not by any means cut as good a figure as the Raja had intended, for his coach overturned and the *Diwan* arrived in Porbandar covered with bandages. He was also in great pain. But everything went according to plan. It was to be a triple wedding, for an older brother of Mohandas and a boy cousin were also to be married to Porbandar girls. The three boys arrived for the wedding, carried on litters and wearing costly wedding clothes. The strange music of the East accompanied them from the house, which Kaba Gandhi had rented for the occasion, to the booth which had been set up for the elaborate ceremony. There were many prayers, many rites to be observed, following the instructions of elders. Then each boy put sweet cake into the mouth of his bride and she did the same to him. But to Mohandas the girl who had become his companion for life was still a stranger. What really interested him at the moment when this great decision was confirmed—a decision made by other people, but binding forever on himself—was the look on the face of his father. In spite of his accident and the pain he still felt Kaba Gandhi showed the face of a very contented man. His sons were all married. He had done well for his countrymen and for his family and could face death calmly. Death was, in fact, very near.

And for Mohandas, childhood, as he had known it, was suddenly over. He would still live at his old house and go to school, but he was a married man, with a wife who would share that home with him. He was at first more shy of her than of anyone else, but she was to be the first person, apart from his mother, with whom shyness could be overcome. Indeed, so far from being shy with Kasturbai he soon tried to become quite a little bully, by his own account. It was tempting to exert his authority and should have been easy to do so with this girl, who had been brought up in the belief that a wife must obey her husband meekly. But when Mohandas became jealous, insisting that his child-wife should go nowhere without his permission, Kasturbai discovered a strong will of her own. They quarrelled frequently because of this clash between his tyranny and her spirit of independence.

And yet real love grew up between this boy and girl, thrown together by the will of others. Mohandas came to find separation from Kasturbai quite unbearable, especially when she returned for long visits to her parents at Porbandar. From the age of thirteen until he was eighteen the boy was frequently separated from his young wife by these visits, for she spent about half the time during those years at her father's home. And when he was eighteen Mohandas was to face a much longer separation.

Meanwhile his education in Rajkot continued. The headmaster of the High School to which Mohandas had been sent before his marriage liked cricket and physical training. Mohandas disliked both. When he could he took long, solitary walks, unless compelled to take part in games or gymnastics. One day he was to proclaim that physical training was no less necessary than mental training, but that was not his view as a boy. Also his father had become a sick man toward the end of his life and Mohandas felt that he should be at the house to attend to his needs. The gymnastics were at the end of the school day and he asked (at first in vain) to be excused so that he could go to his father.

There was much to interest a growing boy in Kathiawar. From quite early years he had been thrilled by plays—something like our old "mystery plays"—in which good and evil were shown dramatically. He must often have seen, too, the vigorous sword dances of the peasants. They would have worn the usual peasant dress for men in that part of India— a shirt and trousers with a short, frilled tunic. But instead of the usual white these clothes would be colored on ceremonial occasions. The dancers performed in the cool of the evening, barefoot, in the open air, with torches and music. There would have been many stories of brigands and of the lions which are still found in that part of India. There were legends of the past, relating to famous saints and kings who once lived in Kathiawar, people whose monuments are temples or forts or—in the case of the great king Asoka—words of wisdom carved in rock. But the present time, too, had a great interest for the boy who cared so much about truth, for things were beginning to stir in India. In spite of so many Indian princes, most of India was ruled by the British, and even the princes had to obey the British Viceroy. Some thirty years before there had been a great revolt against the British overlords, which had failed after a ruthless war, with great

20

cruelties committed on both sides. The people had long remained crushed, their spirits broken, but now new murmurs were sometimes heard.

People were not merely asking, this time, by what right these foreigners ruled them and treated them as inferiors. They asked themselves how the white men managed to do it. Perhaps, said some, it was the food which white men ate that made them strong and powerful. If Indians were ever to hold their heads up again and feel the self-respect which only free men can feel, perhaps—it was suggested—they must learn from these strangers and find the secret of power.

Now one matter in which Hindus differ very much from Christians is the way they think about food. Laws relating to food—what you can eat and when you can eat it, how it is to be cooked and by whom—are to be found in many religions. The Jews had strict laws which are still kept by millions of Jews all over the world. The Prophet Mohammed laid down similar laws, which are kept by good Muslims. Some sections of the Christian Church have their food rules—such as the Roman Catholic practice of avoiding meat on Fridays —but generally speaking we could safely say that there is a great contrast here between the Christian traditions and the traditions of the Hindus. Hindus vary, of course: some Hindus eat meat, some will eat fish but not meat and many millions are strict vegetarians, living on vegetables with milk or curds. But there is one thing *no* Hindu will eat (if he sticks to his religion) and that is beef, because Hindus consider the cow to be a sacred animal.

At least it is true, too, that most English people are meat eaters and it is also true that most Indians are not. Mohandas and his family belonged to a Hindu sect which was very strict about not killing things and would not eat flesh or fish. But young Mohandas had a friend at school who told him that this was a great mistake. He pointed out that English people were bigger than Indians—which is true, on the average, though there are many physical types to be found in India. But there was a rhyme which schoolboys in that part of India knew and Mohandas had heard it:

Behold the mighty Englishman!
He rules the Indian small,
Because, being a meat eater,
He is five cubits tall.

It so happened that this friend of Mohandas was very strong and a fine runner. All this, he said, was due to the fact that he secretly ate meat, though the truth was that he only managed to arrange about one secret meal a month. This other boy was also very brave; and poor Mohandas, in those days, did not feel that he was brave at all. Perhaps meat gave you courage, too, he thought. His friend said so. Mohandas was afraid of thieves, ghosts and snakes. He was also afraid of the dark, because in the dark he imagined thieves in one corner, ghosts in another and snakes in a third. They would all be coming at him, all at once. Only a light would frighten them all away. Even Kasturbai, his child-wife, did not know of these foolish fears, for another fear Mohandas had was one which most people have—the fear of being despised. It is strange to think that we only know of these things now because Mohandas one day became brave enough to tell us the worst about himself, but that day was still far off.

Yet one person *did* know about these secret fears. The friend who wanted to make him brave and strong by meat eating knew everything. "He would tell me," Mohandas wrote when he was a man, "that he could hold in his hand live serpents, could defy thieves and did not believe in ghosts. All this was, of course, the result of eating meat." So Mohandas was persuaded at last that he should eat the food of the English and that "if the whole country took to meat eating, the English could be overcome."

With religious feeling what it was, meat eating had to be done with great secrecy. Mohandas had his first secret picnic down by a river. They ate goat's flesh—tough, at that—and Mohandas was sick. In bed that night he had horrible nightmares, in which a live goat was bleating inside him. But he told himself that meat eating was a duty. Only this way could he help to defeat the English and make India free. So he persevered and even came to like meat. But there was one serious difficulty. Secret feasts of this kind could only be continued by deceit, and Mohandas, in spite of many lapses, still had this deep respect for truth. He had already discovered that there are "silent lies" as well as spoken ones —deception of another kind—and he began to despise himself. It was all too difficult. He gave up his secret feasts just to avoid further deception, even by silence.

Earlier in his childhood, when Mohandas was only twelve

or thirteen, he had taken (as some young boys do) to secret smoking. Often boys who do this make themselves sick, which is probably a good thing and puts an end to the experiment. Meat made Mohandas sick at first, but not his first cigarettes. He had become so addicted that he had even stolen coppers to buy cigarettes at one time. Like most of us, he was a curious mixture, and his devotion to honesty and truth was often forgotten in those days. What had happened when he was only thirteen seemed bad enough to him when he looked back at it later, but he was much more distressed to recall that he stole something when he was fifteen. He had long since given up smoking. This theft had another, and rather curious cause.

One of his brothers owed some money. The brother had a solid gold armlet and Mohandas chipped off some of the gold to pay the debt. It seems a curious kind of theft, because the object was really the payment of the debt, and debt paying is a form of honesty. As Mohandas gained nothing by it himself, it appears that his real fault was in being too high-handed—using the methods of a thief to bring about an act of justice. That's an interesting thing to consider, and I would say he was wrong, but not so bad as he later believed himself to have been. Even at the time, or very soon after, he was very worried about what he had done. And he felt that he must tell his father.

This, however, he found difficult. Kaba Gandhi had never beaten him and he did not expect to be beaten. But he was afraid of the pain that it might cause the old man. For some

24

reason he thought it would be easier if he wrote his confession on paper. Kaba Gandhi, who was an invalid by then, read the confession sitting up on the wooden plank which he used as a bed. The old *Diwan* said nothing, but the tears ran down his cheeks onto the paper.

The affection between Kaba Gandhi and his son was deep and Mohandas realized that day how great it was. It was one of his last, vivid memories of his father before the old man died, the following year.

Bewildered Student in London

Mohandas was sixteen when his father died. He was not a good-looking boy. Small and slight, with a thin, nervous wiriness, he had large ears, which stood out, and a big nose, thick hair and not much chin. Only his eyes and his well-shaped hands were attractive—two features which revealed a good deal of the boy's character, for the eyes were those of a dreamer, but the hands suggested restless activity.

He had been married for three years, but he was still at

school and had achieved no outstanding success. As nobody knew the depths of his curiosity and the struggles that went on within him he must have seemed a very ordinary boy and quite uninteresting.

After Kaba Gandhi's death the family was very much poorer, but among Hindus there is a great sense of family unity, and even distant relatives will feel that they must help when help is needed. Mohandas was sent to college, but gave up after one term. He was not interested and found it all too difficult. His prospects certainly looked very bad.

Yet there was one wise old friend of his father who seems to have had some confidence in the boy. He even thought that he could be a *Diwan*, as Kaba had been. But times were changing. It had been possible for Kaba Gandhi to be a First Minister with no "book learning," but now rulers wanted trained men. Even a degree in an Indian university would not be enough, said the old friend of the family, because there would be so many university graduates soon. Too many lawyers, too, he said—unless Mohandas studied in England. There was a sort of magic about the traveled Indian who had studied abroad—especially in England. It was like the reason for the secret meat eating: by going to England, and studying there, a young man must surely learn some of the things which made the English so powerful.

Mohandas, who had once hoped to defeat the English by eating their food, listened eagerly. But there was still the question of money, and everything seemed to depend on an uncle at Porbandar. So off went Kaba Gandhi's youngest son along the road that he had taken to his wedding. He started by bullock wagon, but decided later to cut the five days' journey short by hiring a camel. It was his first camel ride and must have been very uncomfortable, but he was too excited to worry about that. In four days he arrived at the White City by the Sea.

The uncle at Porbandar was to recommend Mohandas to an Englishman, Mr. Lely, who had an important Government post. Then it was hoped that Mr. Lely, who was believed to have a good opinion of the Gandhi family, would recommend that the former *Diwan's* son should receive some state help in consideration of the past services of the Gandhi family. It was all rather roundabout, but in Eastern countries affairs are often arranged this way. It didn't work, however. This uncle was not at all pleased with the idea of Mohandas going to England. He had known Indian lawyers who had studied law in London and it was a terrible thing to see them dressing like Englishmen, smoking cigars and even eating all the forbidden foods. Mohandas went to see Mr. Lely, with some carefully rehearsed speeches all ready in his mind, but the Englishman just told him to get his B.A. and to come back when he had it.

Back in Rajkot, Mohandas tried to find another way of getting to England. But his mother now opposed the idea. She had never liked it; and the attitude of the uncle at Porbandar now convinced her that the whole plan was a bad one, especially when she compared it with what the neighbors said. Naturally she had been asking everybody about England; and what they told her was enough to worry any Hindu mother—in fact a good deal of it was enough to worry almost any mother anywhere. The neighbors not only said that young Hindus who went to England took to eating meat but that they could not live there without strong drink. Others frightened her with stories of young Indians who were "lost" in England.

In spite of all this the boy, supported by his oldest brother, Laxmidas, had his way. The money was found and Mohandas took vows to satisfy the fears of his mother, promising to keep to the principles of his religion. At the school they took a great interest in the journey, because it was not often that a boy from Kathiawar went to study in England. Mohandas was still such a poor, nervous creature that, when they gave him a big "send-off" from the school, he shook and stammered when he tried to read the few words of thanks which he had carefully written out beforehand. Some of those present must have wondered how this young man imagined he could ever be a lawyer, examining and cross-examining witnesses in a court of law!

He left for Bombay with Laxmidas. When he sailed from Bombay to England it was still four weeks to his eighteenth birthday, yet he left behind for years not only his mother and his wife, but a baby son, a few months old. We know nothing of that sad parting. All the excitement of going on this great journey must surely have faded when that moment came.

He could not have known, but he may well have feared, that he would never see his mother again. Kasturbai he loved dearly, too, in spite of their many quarrels. But here he was at Bombay, once more in the midst of excitement and new experiences, boarding the great ship that was to take him thousands of miles to his first great adventure.

Something had happened in Bombay, however, which had depressed Mohandas in a way which it is very difficult to explain to anyone who is not a Hindu. When I spoke of the marriage of Mohandas I mentioned the system of caste. Much has changed in India since those days. One day Mohandas was to have a son who would marry a woman of another caste, but that would have been quite impossible when he was young himself. The castes were very strong. They laid down their own laws and you could not marry without their approval. If you broke the rules of your caste you could be fined. The Government did not make you pay, but you paid, all the same. And the reason you paid was that *the caste would disown you.* That, to any member of a Hindu caste was the last, worst and most terrifying punishment. We speak of a person as being an "outcast;" and though the two words have no connection, the person expelled from a caste was once a real outcast in Hindu society. He had no place in it. Nobody would give him a job or have anything to do with him—in theory, at least. And that was exactly the threat that hung over the man leaving for England.

While he was waiting at Bombay his caste, known as

the *Modh Banias,* had held a meeting there and summoned him to appear before them. No *Modh Bania* had ever been to England and Mohandas was told that his religion forbade voyages abroad. In England, so they had been informed, he would compromise his religion—he would even have to eat and drink with Europeans. In India and Africa all white people are called Europeans—even when they come from America. Mohandas had heard all this before, of course. He had told them at this meeting of his vows, but the elders of the *Modh Banias* in Bombay had swept all his arguments aside. With a courage which must have surprised him, the young man had refused to be bullied. Even when the dreaded sentence—a sort of spiritual and social excommunication—had been passed on him by the *Modh Banias* he had remained outwardly unmoved.

At the last moment he had been almost alone. His brother had returned to Rajkot. Members of his own caste in Bombay had been forbidden to go with the excommunicated boy to the docks to see him off under penalty of a fine. There had even been a last minute hitch about the passage money, for that had been deposited with a brother-in-law in Bombay, for safekeeping, and he had been afraid to hand it over after Mohandas had been turned out of the caste. Only by the timely help of friends in Bombay, who loaned the necessary money, had he been able to carry out his plans.

So there he was at last on the big steamer, dressed in Western-style clothes, such as he had never worn before, all bought in Bombay. Bombay itself—his first experience of a great modern city—must have seemed strange. But the strangeness of Bombay was nothing compared with this unknown world which lay around and before him. He shared a cabin with an older man, an Indian from his own part of the country. They traveled second class, and all the other second-class passengers were English. Mohandas had never seen so many white people together and here he was, quite unused to speaking their language, trying to hide his embarrassment when, occasionally, one of them spoke to him. It was hard enough to understand them, but even harder to reply. During most of the long voyage this unadventurous adventurer hid in his cabin. It was not that he felt seasick. He was just scared of everybody and everything— frightened of the passengers, of the stewards, of the dining saloon where you had to use a knife and fork (which he was not used to doing) and *very* frightened of unknown dishes which might contain meat and cause him to break one of his vows. He lived on sweets and fruits which he had brought with him.

His cabin companion, a lawyer who was much more at home in this strange world, talked to other people and tried to persuade Mohandas to do the same. In vain this lawyer told his young countryman that he must take every opportunity to improve his English and that his shyness must be overcome if he hoped for any success in law. A kindly English passenger also tried to help, but only depressed Mohandas with well-meant but quite inaccurate information.

He assured the young Hindu that he would have to break his vow not to eat meat, because in England it was so cold that one could not live without it.

When Mohandas said that he had heard otherwise the good man replied that he had been listening to lies. "No one," he said, "to my knowledge lives there without being a meat eater." He must have been very ignorant, but his intentions were obviously good; and no doubt in England he gave equally unreliable information about India with the same excellent intentions. His advice had no effect on Mohandas. In spite of his shyness and timidity he had shown himself stubborn with the elders of the *Modh Banias* in Bombay and he was stubborn now with this English adviser. It was, in fact, the beginning of courage—the thing he admired in others, needed so desperately, and felt that he lacked altogether.

At last the big ship docked at Southampton. The young adventurer had arrived. What had he expected to find? He had one white suit, such as people wear in the tropics. It would have been very suitable for the first part of the sea voyage, but Mohandas had carefully kept it in reserve, wearing black clothes when almost everybody wore white. He thought it would be suitable to wear on his arrival. Of course, when he arrived at Southampton in the cool, late September weather, he was the only person in white. This worried him a great deal. He felt that he had begun his stay in England by making a fool of himself; and of all his fears the fear of looking a fool was one of the greatest.

He was lucky in having introductions to other Indians living in England. To one of these, a certain Dr. Mehta, he had sent a telegram when he arrived at Southampton. Mohandas and his cabin companion went straight to London and stayed at a hotel. The young man was still wearing his white suit, as he had not yet recovered his baggage; and Dr. Mehta, when he kindly called at the hotel to welcome the newcomer, could not quite conceal his amusement. (Fashion is so changeable that today Mohandas would have looked less odd than Dr. Mehta, who arrived in a top hat.) Dr. Mehta gave the young man his first lesson on how to behave in England.

After a weekend at the hotel the two Indians moved to furnished rooms. The excitement of arrival was already over and suddenly London seemed very large and unfriendly, also terrifying. At night Mohandas gave himself up to tears as he lay awake, thinking of his mother—for it was her love that he missed most in this new, bewildering life. And ahead of him, he knew, lay three years of it. He could not turn back now.

Dr. Mehta proved to be a good friend and wise in his advice. "We come to England," he said, "not so much for the purpose of studies as for gaining experience of English life and customs. And for this you need to live with a family." It was the right kind of advice for any young person in any strange country. But the good doctor realized that this young man from Kathiawar was not yet ready for the experience. First he must live with another Indian in London, a man used to English ways but able to understand any difficulties which Mohandas might have.

The advice was gratefully accepted and the young man was introduced to another Indian who treated him like a brother. For a month they shared lodgings at Richmond. They talked English, so that young Gandhi could become familiar with the language, and English ways were explained to him. There was just one difficulty: the food. The landlady simply did not know what to give a young man who would not eat meat or fish. His new Indian friend had quite adapted himself to the usual sort of food to be found in an English house and he tried to reason with Mohandas. "What is the value," he asked, "of a vow made before an illiterate mother, and in ignorance of conditions here?" He said it was pure superstition and added: "You confess to having eaten and relished meat. You took it when it was absolutely unnecessary, and will not where it is quite essential." But the young man who had made a vow prayed for strength to keep it.

At the end of a month Mohandas left Richmond, feeling ready to face life in a London home. Dr. Mehta suggested that he should come nearer now to the heart of London, so a family was found in Kensington, where he now stayed. His regular studies had not yet begun, so he had the whole day to talk, read English newspapers and wander round the great city. He must have seen many places of interest and he began to know London, but what he was really looking for was a vegetarian restaurant, as he heard that such places existed, even in this great English capital where everybody tried to make him eat meat and assured him that it was "essential." At last he found one of these restaurants. He also discovered that many books had been written on the subject of food, and what had once been only a matter of loyalty to a vow became part of a lifelong interest in health. He was to have many interests in the years ahead, but this was one of the earliest and it was permanent. As other interests developed and multiplied his great problem would always be that of strength for doing more and more work. But for the moment no such problem faced him. On the contrary his mind was set on what he afterward described as "playing the English gentleman."

It struck him later as a very funny phase in his life—and, indeed, it was. He bought new and more fashionable clothes, including a top hat. He even provided himself with evening clothes, bought in Bond Street, and he wore a double watch-chain made of gold. He began to take lessons in dancing, but found that he could not keep time with the music, so he gave it up after six lessons. Indian music is so different, that he next decided he must cultivate an ear for this Western music. He bought a violin and took more lessons; but that, too, proved a waste of time and money. The next experiment was elocution, which somebody had recommended. More money was paid out, this time to a teacher who recommended the *Standard Elocutionist* edited by a certain Mr. Bell. Mohandas began on elocution by trying to declaim with fervor a speech by William Pitt.

"Mr. Bell," he wrote in later days, "rang the bell of alarm

in my ear and I awoke." He realized that elocution was of no importance to him and that dancing would never make a "gentleman" of him. He had no need to qualify himself for a lifetime in England. As to being a "gentleman," what did it really mean? He would either become a gentleman by character or give up the idea altogether. Even among his teachers, the woman who had been trying to teach him the violin heard with sympathy—and perhaps with a little relief—that he had decided to give up the lessons and sell the fiddle.

For some years to come Mohandas was to remain rather a fop with regard to clothes, but the period during which he tried to acquire Western "accomplishments" lasted only about three months. One curious thing about his life in London was that, even during those months, he kept very careful accounts of every penny he spent. It was also a good habit to form for a man who was one day to handle public funds! But this accountancy had immediate importance, because it soon showed the young man that he was spending twice as much as he could afford. He left the family in Kensington to live more cheaply on his own in rooms. He gave up, as far as possible, using public transport and walked everywhere —which was also much the best way to learn all about London, or any other city.

And at last, having sufficiently improved his English, he began serious study. He worked first for the London "matriculation," which was much harder than the examination he had passed in India, and involved learning Latin and French —both languages being entirely new to him; and in this he was successful, in spite of many handicaps. Then he began to study law, which was the real purpose of his journey to London.

Timid, Tongue-tied Lawyer

To become a lawyer in England, so Mohandas discovered, two things had to be done. First, for twelve terms (that is to say, for about three years), he had to "keep terms;" and "keeping terms" meant attending at least six out of twenty-four dinners held each term at the Inner Temple. It all sounds rather like a ritual, and that was how he regarded it— but as a silly and meaningless ritual. "Eating his terms," he called it; but in fact the rules laid it down that a law student must be present at so many dinners but they did not compel him to eat anything. That was fortunate, for there was so little that young Gandhi could have eaten without breaking his vow—and he was clear in his mind that his mother had intended to ban fish, as well as meat. His people in Kathiawar did not eat fish, or even eggs—so he had ruled them all out and even come to the conclusion that he would be in better health without them.

For each group of four at the tables two bottles of wine were allowed—they were included in the price of these ritual dinners. Mohandas had also vowed not to drink alcohol, so everybody at these dinners wanted him to join his particular group, just in order to share the wine between three people instead of four. He was specially in demand on "grand nights," once a term, when the best wines were served, plus sherry and port.

The other requirement was a little work. Although Mohandas had to attend these dinners for nearly three years, he found that the work could be done in a very short time. He had to pass examinations in Roman Law and Common Law. Very few students ever failed, although he found that one could pass in Roman Law on two weeks' work and in Common Law after two or three months of intensive study. It seemed odd to the young man that he should have come all the way from Kathiawar to do a few months' work and sit at dinner tables every now and then for three years. Even more odd was the thought that anybody in India could possibly be impressed by a "dinner barrister" from London.

He would be returning with no knowledge at all of Hindu Law or Moslem Law or even the statutory laws of the British in India, except where they precisely followed those of Britain.

But all this he put out of his mind for the moment. He had started his course of dinners while working for "matriculation" and when all that was over he decided to use the rest of the time in solid work for the law examinations. He read all the textbooks, although he knew it was easy to pass without doing so. He passed his exams and was called to the Bar in June, 1891. Only two days later he sailed for Bombay again.

Mohandas had much to think about on that return journey. He had read a great deal in London, thought a lot, seen much and met all sorts of people, including distinguished writers and reformers. His interest in religion had broadened and deepened. In Rajkot he had been tolerant of all religions except Christianity. This was because he had heard Christian missionaries abusing his own religion. (He had also noticed that when a well-known Hindu was converted to Christianity he not only took to eating beef but went about in Western clothes, which, as Mohandas said, "got on his nerves.") But in England he had met a Christian who was shocked to hear about the missionaries in Kathiawar. This man had persuaded Mohandas to read the Bible. He had found most of the Old Testament boring and unpleasant but had come to the Gospels with sudden and quite unexpected delight. In the

Sermon on the Mount he had found his own deepest convictions superbly stated—a complete way of life which he had never thought of as "Christian" because he had never met a Christian who attempted to follow it!

He had even been to Paris, at the time of the Great Exhibition of 1890, when the Eiffel Tower was built, and for days he had wandered through the Paris streets. There would be a lot for the traveler to tell on his return. But how would he be received in Rajkot? He was no longer a *Modh Bania*. They had thrown him out. Would he even be allowed to earn a living, in spite of his London qualifications? And what were they really worth? He had had no practical experience of the courts. He was as shy as ever. On the few occasions when he had been asked to speak in public he had still laboriously written out his little speech and then—even worse—been so overcome with confusion that he could not deliver it! He had even been made a member of the Executive Committee of the Vegetarian Society, which had several distinguished members; but on the one occasion when he had urgently wanted to say something at a committee meeting he had been far too nervous to do so. He had written a statement, which had been read by somebody else. Even on the eve of his departure, at a farewell dinner with his friends, he had broken down in his efforts to make a short and simple speech. What sort of barrister would he make, even if he should be given a chance to practice in the courts?

He felt helpless and afraid. He had no confidence in the goodwill of his countrymen, for he had lost caste; he had even less confidence in himself. There was only one thing he felt he could absolutely rely on: the love of his mother and of his oldest brother, for he was half afraid of his wife still. She would have grown up. She would be a stranger. *And nobody had told him that his mother was already dead.*

Mohandas was a good sailor. Shy as he still was, he did not hide away in his cabin this time, but walked the deck, even in a bad storm which drove almost all the other passengers below. The strong winds and his sense of perfect health when others were unable to stand up to the weather may have done something to calm his mind. The storm was still raging when the S.S. *Assam* arrived at Bombay; but in the mind of the young lawyer there was an almost unnatural calm. He had passed beyond worrying about his difficulties.

His oldest brother, the good Laxmidas, was at Bombay to meet him. Dr. Mehta, his first friend in London, had returned to Bombay and it was at Mehta's house that Mohandas heard of his mother's death. This news, which had been deliberately held back in order that he might not have to face such a disaster in distant London, was a terrible shock. It was even sadder than the death of his father. But he was a man now and made it a point of honor not to show how deeply he felt this loss.

At Rajkot husband and wife met again. It was nearly four years ago that they had parted—Mohandas still a youth, and Kasturbai still a girl, although a mother already. We know as little about their meeting as we know about their parting, but we do know that the gap between them had become wider. Kasturbai, when she was first married, could neither read nor write. That sort of education was not considered necessary for girls. A girl must learn how to cook, to look after a house and to please the man who would be her husband. As a schoolboy Mohandas had tried to teach Kasturbai to read and write, but she had not been interested and he had not been very successful. Later on tutors were engaged, but without much to show for their trouble. Her husband, on the other hand, returning from Europe with all his new knowledge and experience, felt more than ever that they were strangers to each other. But one thing, unfortunately, remained the same in spite of long absence and the utterly different lives they had led: the young man was as jealous and possessive as he had been in his boyhood. And, fortunately—for the sake of them both—the young woman was still determined to assert her right to some independence. They were both stubborn characters.

The trouble with the *Modh Banias* proved to be less disastrous than it might so easily have been. The *Modh Banias* were split: some of them agreed to admit the young man into caste membership again and some were against it. This division was to continue, so that it was never finally settled— some said Mohandas had lost caste and others that he had been admitted into membership again on his return from England. But in the years to come this was to matter less and less, as we shall see. For the moment, however, he had to face the fact that many members of his caste, even if they did not personally dislike him, felt so strongly about what he had done that they considered it wrong even for his own family to have anything to do with him.

It was soon clear that there was little or no work for the inexperienced young lawyer from London. Instead of being made Chief Minister in one of the Kathiawar States, he was not even wanted, at first, for small business in his own town. On the advice of friends he returned to Bombay, to study Indian law and obtain some experience in the High Court. He read Indian Law, much of it with interest, and at last he was asked to appear in court in a small case.

The result was shattering. The moment he stood up in court his head reeled and he was completely tongue-tied. He sat down and another lawyer took over the case, which was really a very simple and easy one. Mohandas, of course, returned the fee he had been paid. He thought of giving up law and taking to teaching instead. At least it was useless to stay any longer in Bombay, for he had earned nothing and the whole family was being involved in debt through his failure. Laxmidas, who had expected so much from his younger brother, had already been allowing the household expenses to become too heavy while Mohandas was still in London.

So the young lawyer returned to Rajkot. The way of living in his home had changed since his father's days. Even while Mohandas was in England his brother had made some alterations to suit the tastes of a young man who would be returning with English habits. Tea and coffee had come into use, crockery had replaced the metal bowls and trays used in a

47

typical Indian home. Most Indians go barefoot or wear sandals, but boots and shoes were worn in the family now. Mohandas himself wore European clothes. All these changes were costing money, with very little coming in (for Laxmidas did not earn very much).

With the help of Laxmidas, who was popular and had useful local connections, the young man at last began to make a living. Laxmidas was in partnership with another lawyer. He now realized that his brother was quite hopeless in a really important case, which would involve appearance in court and the cross-examination of witnesses. But for small jobs, such as applications to be drafted on behalf of poor clients, Mohandas was good enough. In spite of his costly stay in London he was a failure. He knew that, and so did everybody else. But he was not quite a dead loss.

Laxmidas had at one time been secretary to the heir of Porbandar State, before he came to the throne. And Laxmidas was accused of having given this man bad advice—or so the British Political Agent said. (The British had a Political Agent at the Court of every Indian Prince, and the Political Agent was really, of course, more powerful than the Prince himself, because he represented the authority of the British Viceroy.) When this Political Agent was in England Mohandas had met him. Hearing of this, Laxmidas thought it would be a good idea if his brother went to Porbandar and put in a good word for him with the Political Agent. It was very unsafe and bad for business if an Indian, practicing law, was on bad terms with such a powerful person.

Mohandas did not like the idea. If his brother was really at fault, what was the use of his saying anything? If he was not, why couldn't he write in the usual way and present his case? But Laxmidas argued that things were not done that way in Kathiawar. "Only influence counts here," he said, "it is not proper for you, a brother, to shirk your duty when you can put in a good word about me to an officer you know."

So Mohandas set out for the "White City," much against his will. He must have remembered that other journey from Rajkot to Porbandar, when "influence" was the object, and how completely these roundabout tactics had failed. His fears were soon confirmed. The British official remembered having met him in England but could not see why this chance acquaintanceship should now be used for what looked to him like back-door intrigue. He told Mohandas that he had no time to listen.

"If your brother has anything to say," concluded the Political Agent, "let him apply through the proper channel." It was exactly what Mohandas had thought himself—and had said to Laxmidas. But he was here and loyalty made him try to continue. The Agent rose to his feet.

"You must go now."

"But please hear me out . . ."

The white man was really angry now. He called a servant to show his unwanted visitor to the door. The visitor, however, still hesitated, desperately trying to fulfil his mission. The servant seized him by the shoulders and pushed him through the door.

49

In all his reading and thinking Mohandas had been impressed by the idea of *ahimsa*—non-violence. He had admired people who did not retaliate when injured and did not resort or appeal to force. But just now he was too angry and humiliated to think of all that. He wanted to bring a legal action against the Political Agent for assault.

No action was taken, but the reason at the time had nothing to do with the religious principles so much admired by the young lawyer. He sought the advice of a famous Indian lawyer who happened to be in Rajkot. The older man knew, too well, that however good the case might have been (and it was far from being a very good one) the chance of an Indian winning a legal action against a British official before a British Court was too small to be worth considering. On the contrary, it could have disastrous effects for the Indian, because the British would remember it against him that he had dared to bring such an action. So the famous lawyer told Mohandas that such occurrences were common experiences in his profession. The young man, he said, would do better to pocket the insult. This message was brought to Mohandas by a friend, who was told to warn young Gandhi that he would very likely ruin himself and would certainly gain nothing by legal action.

He was not only a failure as a lawyer but he was very unhappy. He felt that even men with far more ability than he believed himself to possess could not be successful in Kathiawar without the help of corruption and intrigue. There were exceptions of course. One of his old schoolmates was

50

soon to rise to the highest public office in the little state of Bhavnagar without stooping to corruption or intrigue. That was Prabhashankar Pattani, whose name was to be honored throughout India as that of a man of fearless honesty and excellent judgment. But Mohandas was probably right about most of the states. He not only lacked confidence in himself, but was quite sure that the way to a state appointment or to success in a legal practice was even more roundabout than this trading on friendship and acquaintance. Simple bribery had a lot to do with it, and if he now rejected even the effort to "pull wires," as he had attempted to do at Porbandar, he was even more clear about his rejection of downright dishonest methods. So everything was against his prospects in Kathiawar, including the fact that he had now made a powerful enemy in this British Political Agent at Porbandar. For, although no legal action had been taken, this man knew that he had threatened to do so; and his hostility could easily wreck a young lawyer.

Then the unexpected happened. Ever since 1860 Indians had been going to South Africa, for work on the sugar estates and for other agricultural purposes in Natal. About fifteen years later Indian merchants had begun to arrive, and some other Indians, formerly laborers, had taken to trading. There were also big firms in India which traded with South Africa, and it was one of these big firms which suddenly offered Mohandas Gandhi an opportunity at a moment when he was more than willing to accept it.

He did not know that his acceptance was to change the

51

whole course of his life. And nobody, perhaps, will ever know why the offer was made at all. The Indian firm was claiming very large damages—in a big law suit. They already had the best lawyers available working on the case, but for some reason they now wanted the help of this funny little man in Rajkot who had started with so little promise—the lawyer who went dizzy when he faced a court and could not even read a carefully prepared speech!

It is one of the oddest things in Gandhi's odd life, and all the more so because of all that came out of it. Did some genius in the Indian firm see the real possibilities that nobody else had yet discovered in Mohandas—not even Mohandas himself? Whatever the reason, they chose him, rather than any of the smart young men then available, and offered him a small fee, with first-class return fare and all expenses.

It was a Porbandar firm, and Mohandas soon met one of the partners, a Muslim already known to his brother Laxmidas. He left even more perplexed as to the reason for his being offered the job, because his work in South Africa was not clearly explained to him. But he could not hesitate in accepting the opportunity for escape, with the lure of new experience in a new country.

He now had two children and it meant leaving his wife and them for a whole year. Yet he did not feel the sadness that he felt when he had left for England. He expected the time to be much shorter, of course; but he knew also that leaving his mother had been the hardest thing. It was hard to leave Kasturbai, all the same, because they were beginning to understand one another. But over there, in that unknown land, who could tell whether there might not be a new life for them all, away from the intrigues of Kathiawar? So he started on his second long journey from Bombay. He was not yet twenty-four when he arrived at Durban, now the great port of Natal, but then a sleepy town on the South African coast, where it faces India across the broad Indian Ocean.

The Struggle for Dignity

Mohandas arrived in South Africa wearing a frock coat and a turban—a curious combination of styles. Abdulla Sheth, a brother of the Muslim merchant he had met at Porbandar was there to welcome him at Durban.

In England he had met many friendly white people and even some in India. But here, from the first moment, he felt that the white people disliked Indians. He did not care for the way they looked at him. As to Abdulla Sheth, without actually disliking Mohandas, he did not seem too pleased when he first saw the very odd young man his brother had sent. What use was he and why had he been sent?

Abdulla Sheth did not even trust the young lawyer; but there he was, and one might as well be friendly. The big law suit was to be heard hundreds of miles away, in Pretoria, and while waiting to be sent there Mohandas visited a court at Durban. The magistrate presiding there ordered him to remove his turban, which he refused to do and left the court. He wrote to a newspaper about it and the matter was much discussed. It might seem only a very small affair, and so it was; but it was the beginning of a long struggle and already, before he left for Pretoria, he was publicly attacked in the newspapers.

He discussed the law suit with Abdulla Sheth and his clerks and found that it was all about bookkeeping—a subject about which he knew absolutely nothing. He got a book on it, however, studied it and soon felt that he understood the case. Abdulla Sheth was bringing an action against another Muslim, a relative of his, and Mohandas—to Abdulla's surprise—mentioned the possibility of settling the whole matter out of court. It seemed, after all, the sensible and friendly thing to do, though Abdulla Sheth remained suspicious. He did not trust anybody much, and certainly not his relatives!

A seat had been booked for Mohandas in a first-class compartment for the first part of his journey to Pretoria. But when passengers were settling down for the night journey up into the high, inland plains, railway officials came and told him he must move. It was clear that they objected to a colored man traveling first class, and so did most white passengers.

"But I have a first-class ticket," exclaimed the young lawyer.

"That doesn't matter," he was told. But he refused to move. A policeman was called and the Indian was put on the platform at Maritzburg, with all his luggage. With some of the obstinacy which had more than once shown itself (in spite of his timidity) Mohandas refused to go to the compartment in which he was permitted to travel. The train went on its way. He spent a cold and miserable night at the station and the next morning sent two telegrams—one to Abdulla Sheth and one to the General Manager of the railway. As a result he was assured of a reserved berth for the following evening and Indians at Maritzburg, informed by Abdulla, came to see him. They were sympathetic, but told him that his experience was nothing unusual. Trouble from officials and white passengers was always to be expected by any colored man who dared to travel first or second class. Before he set out on the next stage of his journey, young Gandhi was already beginning to understand this new country to which he had so gladly "escaped" from Kathiawar.

The railway went no further than a place called Charlestown. From there one continued by stagecoach over the high *veld* (open grassland) to the growing town of Johannesburg. There was trouble again. Mohandas had been provided with a ticket for the coach, but was told it was not in order.

57

The reason, of course, was as before: he was not to sit in the coach with the white people. When told that he could sit outside, he reluctantly agreed. He didn't like to give way to injustice, but somehow he must get to Pretoria.

The seat in which he sat was that of the "leader"—the man in charge of the coach. But after some hours of traveling the leader, who had been sitting inside (in the seat reserved for Mohandas) wanted to smoke. Smoking was not allowed inside the coach, so he told the Indian that he wanted his place. He put some dirty sacking down and said that Mohandas could sit there, at his feet. Worse still he called him "Sami," which—as the lawyer had already learned—was one of the unpleasant expressions which many white men in South Africa used when speaking to Indians or about them. To such people all Indians were "samis" or "coolies"—both contemptuous expressions.

Mohandas refused to move and the man attacked him. He was bigger and stronger than the little Indian, but Mohandas hung on and resisted the attempt to dislodge him. The white passengers, watching this unequal struggle, were soon moved to sympathy for the Indian, whatever they may have thought about "coolies" in general. "If he can't stay there," they said, "let him come and sit with us."

The angry white man felt himself defeated by Indian stubbornness and the sentimentality of his own people, so that battle was won, though the bully made grim threats of revenge. Two days of stagecoach travel brought Mohandas to Johannesburg. For the last, short journey to Pretoria he could travel by rail again, but Indian friends assured him that he would have to travel third class. He was in the Transvaal now—a territory where white people felt even more strongly than their neighbors in Natal about "color." But this time there were agreeable surprises.

The Station Master, who had never before been known to let an Indian buy a first-class ticket (for it was supposed to be against the railway regulations) allowed the smartly dressed lawyer to have one. He could see, he said, that he was a "gentleman." There was one other passenger—white, of course—in the compartment where Mohandas was sitting when the guard came round. It looked as though it was to be a repetition of what had happened before. The guard was for sending him to the third class. He showed his ticket. "That doesn't matter," said the guard. And then the really unusual and unexpected thing happened. The white passenger spoke for him.

"What do you mean," he said, "by troubling the gentleman? Don't you see he has a first-class ticket?"

The guard muttered: "If you want to travel with a coolie, what do I care?" And he went away.

A day was to come when Mohandas Gandhi would not even *wish* to travel first or second class or to dress like a "gentleman." But these early experiences were very valuable. They helped to show him many things—the cruelty and prejudice of people and the underlying decency that would come out at unexpected moments as a reminder that the real struggle was not just a simple affair of white and brown or white and black, but of humanity against inhumanity. And the more he thought about it the clearer it became to him that neither of these qualities had anything to do with the color of a person's skin. The passenger in the train was, in fact, the first of many white people who were to help him.

At Pretoria there was nobody to meet him. It was evening and he needed somewhere to stay the night. He knew that none of the big "white" hotels would accept him. It was just good luck that an American Negro heard him consulting the ticket collector about his problem. As a result he was taken to a hotel owned by an American, where he was able to stay.

Next day he met Abdulla Sheth's English attorney. It seemed that apparently there was very little for him to do in the big law suit. In fact Mr. Baker, the attorney, was much more interested in converting this young Hindu to Christianity. Mr. Baker was a kind man. He had no color prejudice himself and took trouble to find rooms for Mohandas—a difficult thing in a place where there was so much hatred of Indians.

Something had clearly happened to Mohandas since he left Rajkot. The little affair of the turban on arrival in Natal, the Press controversy that followed and the series of incidents on the journey to Pretoria marked a swift awakening; and he followed this up in Pretoria by examining and discussing the position of Indians in that part of South Africa—also suggesting and taking some active steps with regard to Indian interests. He called a meeting of all the Indians in Pretoria (mainly Muslims) and made the first public speech of his life. Because he cared deeply about the matter, his shyness seems to have vanished suddenly. He took up the case of Indians in correspondence with the railway authorities and obtained from them an assurance that Indians would be allowed to travel first and second class if "properly dressed." This was not quite satisfactory, as it was left to the Station Master to decide whether the clothes of an Indian were "proper." But it was at least a beginning.

He studied the whole position of Indians in the Transvaal carefully and, as a result, did not only criticize white people. Just as a general must look critically at his own troops, if he hopes to win battles, this newcomer knew that it was not enough to complain to or about the white people. In the struggle that lay before them Indians must win respect. He told them bluntly that many of their habits were unsanitary; it was not the real cause of prejudice, but it must increase it— at least with English people—and provide prejudiced minds with a ready excuse. He realized that relations with white people would be much better if Indians all spoke at least one of the two European languages. The majority of whites, descendants of Dutch settlers, spoke *Afrikaans,* a language derived mainly from Dutch. The rest spoke English, a language of which many Indians at least knew a little. The London-trained lawyer, whose English was very good, by Indian standards, offered to teach this language to other Indians and spent some time in doing so to a few pupils.

The boy Mohandas had become Gandhi, the leader of men. Only on a small scale, as yet. But the way he assumed leadership in Pretoria marks a very important stage in his life. And it was not just Hindu leadership. It was as an Indian speaking to Indians that he made his first public appeal, begging the small community in Pretoria to forget whether they were Hindus, Muslims, Parsis or Christians in considering their common problems.

Indians in the Transvaal, he found, were made to pay a special tax on admission into the country, which was dominated by the settlers of Dutch origin, known as Afrikaners. Indians could not own land. They had no votes. Like the Negro people, who formed the vast majority of the population, they were not allowed out after nine o'clock at night without a pass and they were not allowed to walk on the pavement.

In his new mood the young lawyer was not disposed to accept this humiliation of walking always in the gutter, to satisfy the pride of the white men. One day he was with an English Quaker who was very friendly toward him when he was violently attacked, without warning, by a white policeman for walking on the pavement. The Englishman was horrified. He offered to be a witness if Mr. Gandhi brought a legal action for assault. But Mohandas said there was no need. The "poor man," as he called the policeman who had kicked him, no doubt treated all colored people that way.

"I have made it a rule," he said, "not to go to court in respect of any personal grievance." He had already gone a long way since, so recently, he wanted to prosecute the Political Agent at Porbandar!

"Just like you," said his friend. It was already the sort of thing one would expect from this strange young man. The English Quaker spoke to the policeman and Gandhi did not understand what he said, because the policeman was an Afrikaner and they spoke in Afrikaans. Surprisingly the policeman then apologized—"for which," Gandhi wrote later, "there was no need. *I had already forgiven him.*"

Meanwhile Gandhi had been studying carefully the big law suit which had brought him to South Africa. He saw that Abdulla had a very strong case, but he also saw that the cost of this case was going to ruin both parties. It was stupid for two men from distant Porbandar to be fighting an action here which would ruin them both—two Muslim Indians, and relatives at that! He persuaded them to submit the whole thing to arbitration by somebody whom they could both trust. As a result Abdulla Sheth won; but the young lawyer's task of reconciliation did not end there. He next persuaded Abdulla to deal leniently with the other man, not demanding the whole sum owing to him at once, but accepting smaller payments over a very long period, to save his rival from bankruptcy. Both men had good reason to be grateful to him. He had entered into the case an unknown and very un-successful lawyer, totally ignorant of the country and the subject of the dispute; he brought it to a successful con-clusion which showed him able to succeed by sheer ability to grasp all the facts, understand the people concerned and negotiate honestly between them. His first success as a lawyer was not a crushing victory over an opponent, but the triumph of good sense and humanity.

He went back to Durban and was about to return to India when a short paragraph in a newspaper led him to make a decision that was to change his whole life. Indians in Natal had been, in many ways, better treated than those who had gone into the Transvaal. They could own land and they had even been allowed to vote in the elections. The paragraph that caught Gandhi's attention said that a bill was to be brought before the Natal Legislative Assembly to deprive Indians of this right to vote.

He discussed the matter with the Indians in Durban and they said he must stay another month. "We will fight," they said, "as you direct us."

Again he seemed to be acknowledged as a leader. Old Abdulla thought it was a good idea. "But you should remember," he told the others, "that he is a lawyer. What about his fees?"

"*Abdulla Sheth, fees are out of the question.*" Was it little Mohandas speaking? No, this was the new Gandhi. "There can be no fees for public work," he said. Others must help, too—voluntary workers. But a campaign could not be conducted without money. There would be literature to publish, correspondence, telegrams, traveling expenses, law books to be bought and many other costs.

His generous offer caught the imagination of the Muslim

merchants. "Allah is great and merciful," they cried. "Money will come in. Men there are, as many as you may need."

So what was to have been a farewell party suddenly became a working committee. The first campaign of Gandhi had begun. They brought in the Indian Christians—many of them better educated than most Indians in South Africa, but until that time despised by the Muslim merchants. All barriers between the great religions were wiped out as the Indians set to work for a common purpose—the Christians, in particular, delighted to find themselves suddenly treated with so much respect by other Indians.

Probably this campaign started much too late to stop a bill which was within a few days of becoming law. Perhaps it could never have succeeded, anyway. Gandhi himself had not expected success, but he was delighted at the new spirit among the Indians of Natal. There seemed, for the moment, to be little more that he could do, and once more he was on the point of returning to India. But this time his fellow countrymen in Durban begged him to stay. Twenty merchants offered to employ him as a lawyer. The grateful Abdulla said he would furnish a house for him. They were not to be resisted and Gandhi agreed to stay.

Natal, though an easier place for Indians than the Transvaal, had already become harder with the abolition of the Indian right to vote. In his own profession of law Gandhi now met another example of white prejudice, for the Law Society of Natal tried to prevent him from practicing in the courts. He won the struggle with the Law Society; but the

Chief Justice, who gave his ruling in favor of the young lawyer, told him to remove his turban. Not long ago he had left a magistrate's court rather than do that, but now it seemed to him a matter not worth argument. He had become interested in much more important things than the right to wear a turban. Now that he had found strength of character he knew it should be used for bigger battles and better causes. He had taught Sheth Abdulla how and when to compromise, and now he could apply compromise to his own affairs. He did not even mind now if people criticized him for giving way. The man who had learned to be sure of himself and proved his courage and determination no longer felt that terror he had once known of being laughed at or thought weak and foolish.

So the victory over the Law Society was not spoiled by what most white people would have thought a childish gesture of defiance. And, as a result, the newspaper comments were mainly favorable, supporting the Judge who had rejected the case of the jealous and selfish white lawyers. And this was very important, because the real reason that kept Gandhi in South Africa was his desire to help his fellow countrymen there; and to do this he needed as many friends as possible among the white people.

He had enough legal business to make a good living, but not enough to prevent him from giving a great deal of time to voluntary work for his people. Already in India there existed an Indian National Congress to work for Indian rights, and now Gandhi founded the Natal Indian Congress for the same purpose in this South African colony. It was built up with the money of the wealthier Indians; but Gandhi, who was Secretary of it, knew that the ones most needing help were the poor laborers. They had come because they were poor, with no land and no work in their own country; and before they came they had all been made to agree to a contract promising five years' work for a white employer. They could be severely punished if they tried to leave their jobs before the five years were up, and during that time many were treated little better than slaves. In Gandhi they now found a champion if they were beaten or ill-treated. He did not try to get the white masters punished but he did use all his legal knowledge to help the wretched laborers. He could not understand why so many white people rejoiced in humiliating these laborers—it was a mystery to him, he said, how men could feel themselves honored by this sort of behavior.

At the end of another two years he realized that this was where his work now lay. Not merely his work as a lawyer, though he had built up a good practice, but his work for his fellow countrymen, because so many of them needed him. But it was now three years since he had seen his wife and his two children. If he was to make his life in South Africa it was time to bring his family from Rajkot. So, for a while, he returned to India.

Quiet, Dignified Resistance

It was the second big reunion of the Gandhi family, and
once more we know nothing of what passed when they were
reunited at Rajkot. Gandhi remained about six months in
India, spending most of his time in efforts to interest people—
English as well as Indian—in the plight of the Indians in
South Africa. Even in his own country he had to suffer
humiliations on account of his color. A friendly English
journalist took him to an English club in Calcutta and was

very embarrassed to discover that he could not take the Indian lawyer into the drawing room. That was only for white people. But an event like that was nothing compared with the things that Gandhi had seen and suffered in South Africa.

When there was an outbreak of plague in Bombay, and fear that it would spread to Kathiawar, he offered his services to the Sanitation Department at Rajkot. He spent some time inspecting houses and advising on ways to keep them more clean and healthy, as the best precaution against disease. It was not a pleasant job, but he had found that he could do unpleasant things if they were necessary to the community. Also he learned a good deal, finding that the most poor and downtrodden people were, on the whole, the cleanest and the most willing to have their houses inspected.

The brother-in-law in Bombay who had refused to let Gandhi have his passage money for the journey to England, because he was so terrified of the *Modh Banias,* was very ill. Gandhi had no bad feelings about him. He took him to Rajkot and nursed him there, staying with him day and night, though he was trying himself to write about South Africa at the time. The patient died, however, and Gandhi adopted his son, who sailed with the Gandhi family when the young leader was urgently asked to return to Natal.

On the way there was a very bad storm. As usual, Gandhi was among the few who were not sick, though the ship was in real danger and most of the passengers, unused to sea

70

voyages, were terrified. He did his best to help and encourage them all.

At last, to the great relief of the frightened passengers, the storm ended; and soon afterward the ship reached Durban. There was some delay before the passengers could land, as they had come from Bombay and there was danger of the plague being brought to Natal, but after some days it was decided that the passengers could safely be allowed ashore. They brought no danger to Natal, but danger was waiting for at least one of them.

False reports of what Gandhi had said about Natal during his visit to India had been spread, and most white people in Durban were very angry. He was advised to go ashore after dark, but he chose to go openly by daylight. Kasturbai and the children were driven to the place where they were to spend their first night in South Africa. Gandhi followed on foot, with an English friend, and was soon surrounded by a mob of white people. Separated from his English friend, he was stoned and kicked. Fortunately the wife of a British Superintendent of Police came that way and with great courage stepped between Gandhi and the mob. An Indian boy ran to inform the Superintendent himself, and Gandhi was escorted, the rest of his way, by police. He refused an offer to take refuge in the police station and went on to the house of a friend, where his wife and the children were waiting for him.

Once more there was danger, as an angry crowd soon collected round the house. They wanted to "hang old Gandhi on a sour apple tree," and it looked as though they might break in, doing great damage to others, besides Gandhi. The Police Superintendent, realizing this, sent a message to Gandhi, strongly urging that he should escape in disguise. Gandhi did so and was never quite sure afterward whether he had done the right thing or not. If it was right to escape now in disguise, was it right to have insisted on walking the streets by day instead of being smuggled ashore at night? And if it was wrong to take refuge in the police station, after his rescue from the mob, how could it be right to go there— as he did—after his escape, in disguise, from the house?

He was the kind of man who would worry himself about that sort of thing for years, because it was so important to find the right thing and stick to it. The important thing at the time, however, turned out to be neither his caution nor his courage but the fact that he had no malice toward his persecutors. After his escape from the house the Police Superintendent told the crowd that they had been hoaxed. He said two of them could come into the house with him to make sure, and that if they found Gandhi there they could do what they liked with him. So the crowd soon realized how cleverly they had been tricked and went home; and by the next day many people were wondering what would happen as a result of this cowardly attack by a white mob on one little Indian.

They were not left long in doubt. Gandhi declared publicly that he did not want to prosecute anybody. He saw no use— even if a "white" court would have convicted those who were guilty—and he said the people who had attacked him were not to blame—they had believed an incorrect cable by the Reuter press agency about his speeches in India. Patiently he explained what he had said and what he had not said in India, and the papers published his statement, together with the news that he would not prosecute anybody. The white people began to think very differently about him after that.

In many small ways Gandhi was changing, and some are worth noticing at this point. He still had to "keep up appearances," as a lawyer who attended the courts, but his life was becoming simpler. With so much need around him he did not like to spend money unnecessarily on himself. He took to washing his own clothes and did it so badly at first that other lawyers laughed at him. Once that would have seemed a terrible thing, but now he said that if he could save money and give other people amusement, too, it was an additional advantage!

Another day he came to court with an extraordinary haircut and the other lawyers asked if rats had been gnawing his hair. No, he told them. The white barber would not condescend to cut his black hair, so he had cut it himself. And then he thought of the downtrodden "Untouchables," the dregs of Hindu society in his own country. Who could blame the white barber? Were not caste Hindus just as cruel to their own countrymen?

In 1899 war broke out between the Afrikaners and the British Government. It was called the Boer War, because most of the Afrikaners were Boers (farmers). They were strong in the Transvaal and in the Orange Free State (where no Indians were allowed) but in Natal most of the white people were British.

What ought Gandhi to do—or the other Indians? Neither of the two white nations had treated the Indians well, though the Afrikaners, as we have already seen, had so far behaved more harshly toward them, on the whole. And Gandhi's gentle nature could not readily accept the idea of helping in a war, anyway. But among many confusing facts one thing seemed, at the time, to be clear to him: he believed in the British, hoped much from them and considered it his duty to support them. He raised an ambulance corps of over a thousand Indians and, when they had trained, they went to the war, where they served under fire and marched twenty to twenty-five miles a day, carrying the wounded men on stretchers. In later years Gandhi recalled with happiness a march on a hot day with Indian stretcher-bearers and British soldiers. They had halted at a very small stream and each party had wanted to give way to the other as to which should drink first.

Once more Gandhi thought his work in South Africa had ended, and he returned to India with his family when he was thirty. Expensive gifts were made to him by the grateful Indians of Natal, but he felt that he could not keep them. Service must be its own reward, and valuable ornaments had no place in a house of such simplicity as his. Besides, he had been telling other people that they did not need such things! So all the gifts were handed to trustees, to be sold for the community. It meant a difficult argument with his wife, but Gandhi had his way; and, in the end, Kasturbai came to agree with him.

Gandhi did not remain long in India, though he began, once more, to have success as a lawyer—just as he had done in South Africa. When he was suddenly and urgently asked by his friends in Natal to return he still thought it could only be for a short time. He left his wife and children behind, expecting to rejoin them soon in India. It was near the end of 1902 when he sailed, for the third time, from Bombay to Durban.

He found that his real work was in the Transvaal. After the defeat of the Boers, and the overthrow of their Republic, the Transvaal was, for the moment, ruled by the British. They had promised that things should be better for Indians, but in fact they were as bad, or even worse. It was much harder, even, for Indians to get into the Transvaal at all. Gandhi himself only obtained a permit to go to the Transvaal through the help of his old friend, the British Police Superintendent at Durban. The British had set up a new Government Department in the Transvaal to deal with Indians and other Asians. The men in charge were British officials, most of whom had served before in India and other British possessions in Asia. Gandhi found them more unfriendly and unfair than the white officials of the old Afrikaner Republic. The new department, so far from helping and protecting Indians, was clearly hostile to them— except for the few who obtained concessions by bribery.

75

His first big effort to help his fellow countrymen in the Transvaal was to collect evidence of bribes received by British officials in the "Asiatic" Department of the Government. The Police Commissioner, who was a just man, agreed, after examining Gandhi's witnesses, that he was right. But it would be difficult in South Africa, he said, to get a white jury to convict white men for offenses against colored men. Gandhi knew this, but he selected the two worst offenders and warrants were issued for their arrest. The British officials were informed of all this by spies, and before the arrests could be made one of them tried to escape. He was arrested and brought back. In spite of his guilty flight from justice and strong evidence of bribery, he was found not guilty. So was the other. Gandhi began to lose faith in the law. What was the use of being a lawyer if the courts protected such people? And yet he had not failed, for the cases had much publicity and the Government dismissed the two men concerned.

The Indians rejoiced, but Gandhi himself never enjoyed the humiliation of other people. The two men appeared to face ruin. They tried to get work with the local authorities in Johannesburg, and were told that they would be appointed only if Gandhi did not object. So he was reckoned a force in this country, though he held no office! When asked if he would oppose the employment of these men he said he would not. It was rather like his first case in Johannesburg, where he had won a cheap victory for Abdulla Sheth and then persuaded him to be generous with his defeated rival. Other

British officials, noticing this, felt more friendly to the little Indian lawyer. However much he might struggle with them, they knew that he was really a friendly person, who wished harm to nobody.

In 1904 a new Indian paper began to appear weekly in South Africa. It was called *Indian Opinion*. Gandhi was not the editor, but for the first two years he had to do most of the work. Also, as it was published at a loss, he had to find the money for the weekly losses, which were sufficient to keep him poor, in spite of his good legal practice. The paper provided another means to make the wealthier Indians more interested in the difficulties of the poor Indian laborers. (Gandhi was known to all Indians in those days as "bhai," which means "brother," and it gave him great pleasure to hear this name, especially when the laborers used it.) Almost from the beginning *Indian Opinion* was printed near Durban, at a place called Phoenix Settlement, later handed over to a public trust. Here Gandhi had bought land so that settlers of any race could come and live by cultivating the soil and working at the printing press. Owing to his work, hundreds of miles away at Johannesburg, he was at first unable to spend much time at Phoenix, a pleasant place in slightly hilly country, but Kasturbai and his family were often there after they rejoined him in South Africa.

This settlement had to be in Natal, because in the Transvaal it was not possible for Indians to own land; and Gandhi spent much of his time in legal disputes over efforts to turn the Indians out altogether. He lived in a suburb of Johannesburg, rising always very early, helping with all sorts of work in the house—for he believed that all should take their share in such work—and walking every day to his office and back. That meant ten miles of brisk walking every day.

Gandhi was living for the service of his countrymen and mainly living among them, though his legal and political work made him familiar, too, with white people—lawyers, officials and others. A few white people were to become his close friends and work with him. Among the others he had always found at least a few who respected him; and even in Johannesburg the respect for Gandhi, as a man, steadily increased among the white people who knew him. But the vast majority of the population, the Negro people, who were even more helpless than the Indians and worse treated, hardly crossed his path. Then, in 1906, the Zulus in Natal rebelled. It was a hopeless revolt from the beginning and it was soon ruthlessly crushed by the well-armed white people. But it gave Gandhi a chance to look, for a moment, beyond the conflict of Indian and European interests into the deeper conflict of the African Negroes with the white settlers who had complete power over them, yet feared their revenge for all that they had suffered.

In this struggle, which was to become more intense and bitter in the years to come, the Zulu Rebellion was one of the small beginnings. Gandhi saw it as a stretcher-bearer, marching once more with his Indian volunteers, this time up to forty miles a day through hilly country. They nursed the

Zulus, who were not, as he expected, men wounded in battle but friendly tribesmen who had been shot by mistake, and others who had been savagely flogged, causing festering sores. The "rebellion," Gandhi discovered, consisted mainly of a refusal to pay a new tax imposed on the Zulus by the white people and in the murder of a white official. For this soldiers were sent to terrify the Zulus into submission. "My heart was with the Zulus," Gandhi said, when he wrote of the "rebellion" later. The British soldiers, who had caused the suffering, would do nothing to relieve it, and some of them, at first, even tried to stop the Indians from going to the help of "these innocent people" (as Gandhi regarded them) with bandages and disinfectants. Later, however, Gandhi managed to make himself understood to the white soldiers and they stopped interfering. Some of the officers even thanked him.

It was not a war, he realized, but a man hunt. Many English people privately shared his opinions. He was glad that he and his small band—only twenty-four, this time—had come, because the Zulus had been so grateful. And he knew that, but for the Indians, the Zulus would have been without help. The British Medical Officer had admitted that. But if any thought of further service among the Zulus ever crossed his mind, the urgent need for his presence in Johannesburg must have put such ideas out of his mind.

Indeed, the plain truth was that most white people in the Transvaal at that time feared the Indians more than they feared the Negro people, whom they could still treat like cattle. The Englishman at the head of the "Asiatic" Department told Gandhi: "It is not the vices of Indians that Europeans in this country fear, but their virtues." The white people were therefore determined to drive the Indians out of the Transvaal and new measures against them were already being considered. Gandhi and another Indian were sent to London, in order to persuade the British Government to prevent such measures; but the British had already decided on "self-government" for the Transvaal. This meant, of course, government by the white minority—mostly Boers. One of the Boer leaders, General Smuts, said plainly that "the Asiatic cancer" as he called the Indians, ought to be rooted out of South Africa.

Smuts belonged to the party which won the first election held after the Boer War, in 1907. Then the storm broke. The first of the new anti-Asian laws included the compulsory registration of every Asian over the age of eight years with his or her fingerprints, as though they were all criminals. They had all been registered once and many felt that they might as well resist now as wait until things became worse. Since, like the Africans, they had no votes and therefore no responsibility for the laws, what did the law mean to them? Gandhi, who had explained to his community that resistance would not be easy, began to feel a new confidence now, as he sensed the determination of his people. But he warned them that just disobeying the Government would not be enough. They must have no hatred in their hearts and they must cast out fear. He and his friends began using, for the first time, a new word—*satyagraha*—meaning the force or firmness of truth.

A number of Indians and a prominent Chinese were sentenced to imprisonment for defying the new law. They offered no defense in court—they all pleaded guilty to breaking the "Black Act," as they called it, by failure to register. Gandhi was among the second batch. The magistrate who sentenced him had a great respect for him. Gandhi got only two months' imprisonment and complained that those whose offense was less than his, as a leader, had been treated more severely. There were, of course, jails for white people and very much worse jails for colored people. These soon became overcrowded with Indian resisters. Gandhi was taken out of the jail to see General Smuts, who agreed that the "Black Act" should be repealed if most of the Indians registered voluntarily—a compromise which they had already offered before the Act was passed. Gandhi agreed to recommend this compromise again.

But when this was told to the Indians some of them felt they had been betrayed. Gandhi was now threatened with violence, and even with death, by some of his own people. He himself and some of the leaders were the first to set out for the place where voluntary registration was to take place. A group of Pathans (Muslims from the northwest frontier of India) met them; and while they talked one of the Pathans suddenly struck Gandhi on the head from behind, others kicking and striking him as he lay on the ground. The first thing he thought of, when he regained consciousness, was to stop police proceedings against the men who had attacked him. But, in spite of Gandhi's refusal to give evidence against them, the men were sentenced to imprisonment.

He still had to face the charge of betrayal and even of having been heavily bribed by Smuts. He was again attacked by a Pathan, this time in Natal, where he had gone to explain the position. But the pact with General Smuts was explained through *Indian Opinion;* and the Indians, as a whole, accepted it. Smuts did not; when they had done their part he failed to do his. The "Black Act" was not repealed.

Many of Gandhi's own colleagues who had stuck to him now turned against him. He had been too trustful, they thought. He replied that it was a duty to trust one's fellow men. Gandhi pleaded again with Smuts; but in spite of repeated warnings the Transvaal Government still refused to repeal the Act. Indian resistance was renewed, beginning with a crowded meeting at Johannesburg. The leader of the group of Pathans who had attacked Gandhi had just come out of prison. He knew that Gandhi had refused to take action against him and he could see now that there had been no betrayal. He apologized publicly to the little lawyer and they shook hands. Then all the Indians who had registered voluntarily threw their certificates of registration into a great fire. These certificates were supposed to be carried about like passports, to produce on the demand of the police; so the chief purpose of registration broke down with the destruction of them.

Some Indians from Natal next joined in the struggle. They

openly crossed the border into the Transvaal, where their presence as "unregistered" Indians was illegal. They were arrested and imprisoned. Since licenses to sell goods in the street could only be obtained by producing a certificate, many Indians in the Transvaal sold without a license, openly, and informed the Government. They, too, went to prison, and the prisons were soon overfull, though hardships were inflicted on the prisoners to break their spirits and discourage others from following them.

While this struggle continued the union of South African territories was being discussed in South Africa and in London. Gandhi, of course, was in prison most of this time, but when he came out after his third imprisonment he gave careful thought to the proposed union. It would surely mean, he felt, that the milder laws of Natal and the Cape Colony would be replaced by the much harsher laws of the Transvaal and the Orange Free State. Others agreed that something must be done to stop this, and two Indians were sent to London. Gandhi was one of them.

They failed. Anxious now to please Smuts and the other "Boer" leaders, whom they had recently defeated in war, the British Government agreed to the union without any provision to protect the Indians. Gandhi returned, defeated, to a country where the only "rights" a man could look for, unless he was one of the privileged few who had the vote, were the rights he claimed for himself, in defiance of the law. And that meant suffering.

He made a big decision. He would give up practicing as a

lawyer. You couldn't go on earning your living by the law when you were defying it, and it wasn't even practical any more. From now on he would be in and out of jail—a man living on faith, hope and charity. For years he had been living more and more simply, becoming increasingly interested in manual work—the work which, he realized, was the most essential and at the same time the worst paid and the most despised. He felt that educated Indians should be taught to respect this kind of work and the people who did it. In jail and out of jail he set an example in this, as he did in everything he taught.

So some land was bought near Johannesburg. Though no Indian could own land in the Transvaal, Gandhi had now a number of loyal white friends who were able to help. One was a German architect, called Herman Kallenbach. Gandhi realized that the Phoenix Settlement, in distant Natal, was too far from Johannesburg, the center of the struggle. On land bought by Kallenbach they started a new venture, known as Tolstoy Farm, after the great Russian writer whom Gandhi so much admired. Here people of different nationality, color and religion lived together as brothers and sisters, sharing in the farm work, the carpentry and sandal making and other crafts by which they lived, sharing also the simple comforts which this joint work provided for them, dressing in rough clothes suitable for such work and taking their part in the campaign of *satyagraha* against the Government. If anyone was arrested there were always others to care for his family, since all things at Tolstoy Farm were shared.

Not only men joined in defying unjust laws. Indian women, including Kasturbai, were outraged by a court decision in South Africa that an Indian marriage was not recognized by law. They joined the campaign, openly broke laws and were imprisoned in large numbers.

Among other grievances of the Indians was a tax of £3 (about $15) a year (worth a great deal more, in those days, of course) which was levied on the Indian laborers who came to Natal. The tax was levied on each male member of the family over the age of sixteen and each female member over thirteen, so that a man with a wife and only two children could be paying £12 a year, which Indian laborers in those days could only pay by running heavily into debt. In the coal mines of Newcastle (Natal) the Indian workers went on strike against this tax in 1913. There were more arrests, more imprisonments.

There were soon complaints of flogging and ill-treatment in the prisons. The houses of workers on strike were deprived of light and water. Indians were, in many cases, turned out of their houses by the mining companies, and Gandhi set up a camp for them, supported by money from Indian merchants.

Impressed by the success and orderliness of the strike, the coal owners asked to meet Gandhi. He explained the whole position to them. How would they feel about such a tax? What other way was open to the Indian worker, who had no vote, except to protest by refusing to work? Even the mining officials had begun to show sympathy for these wretched men and women, who had behaved so firmly and yet so peacefully; but there seemed to be no solution in sight. So Gandhi, who had for some weeks been planning this move, set out at the end of October, 1913, with some 6,000 Indians from the mines toward the Transvaal. He publicly announced that he proposed to cross the border, illegally. Thus the homeless Indian miners could, at the same time, challenge the tax which crippled them in Natal and the laws which kept them out of the Transvaal.

In the Transvaal Gandhi was arrested and imprisoned once again. His 6,000 followers were also arrested, but taken back to Natal before they were charged. The reason was clear. Without enough jails to take another 6,000 prisoners, the Government of the South African Union could only solve this problem and—so they hoped—keep the mines working by making the mines into a temporary jail and condemning the men to work there as prisoners! The mines were surrounded by barbed wire and every effort was made to compel the men to work by flogging and otherwise ill-treating them.

It did not work, Gandhi had aroused in them the spirit of quiet, dignified resistance. Soon thousands of other Indians came out on strike to support the heroic Indian miners—men on the sugar estates, workers employed by the townships. Even the guns of the military police failed to break this spirit of inspired resistance, though many were killed or wounded. Among the white people the tide of opinion began to turn as the consciences of many became worried by what was happening.

Faced by an impossible situation, by growing uneasiness among all decent white people and by criticism all over the world, the South African Government gave way on the tax and the "Black Act." General Smuts, defeated in war by the British, had been defeated by unarmed Indians, led by a kindly, friendly little man who made him feel helpless. In July, 1914, his great work in South Africa finished, Gandhi left for London. It was the eve of the First World War.

A New Kind of Leader

Gandhi, with his wife and the faithful Mr. Kallenbach, arrived in London on August 6th, two days after the declaration of war. He went to England at the request of a prominent Indian leader, who was in Europe at the time. Whatever this man's intentions were, the outbreak of war seems to have changed the whole situation.

During most of his stay in London Gandhi was ill with pleurisy, but he appealed to Indians in Britain to offer their services for ambulance work. In his attitude to the war he said that he was "groping in the dark." He regarded war as immoral and considered any assistance—even ambulance work, if undertaken under military orders—as inconsistent with *ahimsa* (non-violence). But as he could not stop the fighting he believed that he had a duty to do something else; and his choice of what to do was, in fact, a typical compromise. He had already shown himself a master of compromise; and whether he was right or wrong his firmness always won respect. Many Indians felt that, quite apart from any question of violence and non-violence, the British were fighting for a freedom which Indians did not share. "We are slaves," they said, "and they are masters. Why should the slave help the master?" Gandhi did not see it that way. He still hoped much from the British, and even more, if Indians could win their gratitude. So much respect was felt for him by the Indian community that a number of young men enlisted for ambulance work.

In the cold, damp English winter Gandhi was very slow to recover. At last he accepted the pressing advice of English friends to return to India where, no doubt, he could find useful work to do. Mr. Kallenbach wanted to go with him, for the good German had become very attached to his Indian friend. But, as a German, he was not allowed to go (because of the war), so the Gandhis went without him. The one thing Gandhi specially noticed about the voyage was that the white people on the ship were so unfriendly. This was curious, because he had never noticed this on many earlier sea voyages between India, England and South Africa. Had things, in fact, become worse? If so it must have seemed a sad blow to Gandhi, who had so recently been pleading with Indians in London not to press their demand for freedom while Britain was in difficulties, but to help as well as they could, even in a war and in spite of all his convictions about violence.

When Gandhi landed at Bombay, in 1915, he had been most of twenty-two years in South Africa, with only two short visits to his homeland. Before that there had been the years in England. The great mass of Indians, who could not read the newspapers, knew little or nothing about him. As to those who had read about him, not all were impressed. Many thought that he was just a crank. But there was quite a crowd of friends and admirers to welcome the Gandhis at Bombay and to throw garlands of sweet-smelling flowers round their necks, as Indians do when they wish to welcome people.

Gandhi was forty-five. He had recovered his health on the sea voyage, and—thanks to regular exercise and careful choice of food for so many years—he had abundant energy. The British Government sensed at once that he could be a valuable friend or a formidable opponent. The British Viceroy gave him a gold medal for his services to the Indian community in South Africa. The Governor of Bombay asked to see him. "I ask one thing," said the Governor. "Come and see me whenever you propose to take any steps concerning Government."

To the old leaders of Indian nationalism Gandhi gave a series of shocks. He had developed ideas about simplicity and humility which did not fit in at all with their picture of a dignified leader. When Gandhi was missing at an Indian institution which he visited, the great Indian leader who was in charge of it asked where his visitor was. He was told that Gandhi was cleaning all the lavatories. There was a special reason for this sort of thing. Caste Hindus despised such work and considered it fit only for "Untouchables." Gandhi was determined to teach by example that all should take their share in humble or unpleasant work and that nobody should be despised for doing things that were necessary to the community. He now traveled third class and wore the simple clothes of a peasant, so that he soon came to understand very well how poor people were treated by officials in his own country, for in those days very few people knew him as he traveled about.

Near Ahmedabad, an ancient town in Gujerat, between Bombay and his own country of Kathiawar, Gandhi made a new home for his family and fellow workers. They lived in what is called an *ashram,* a settlement rather like Phoenix, in Natal, or Tolstoy Farm, in the Transvaal, for they shared in a very simple life, dedicating themselves to the service of God and their country. The idea of an *ashram*—something rather like a monastery in some ways—is something that Hindus understand, for Hindu religious leaders have often lived in this way with their disciples. This new settlement, called the *Satyagraha Ashram,* was very soon moved to a place on the bank of the River Sabarmati—just outside Ahmedabad.

Almost from the beginning Gandhi had "Untouchables" living in his new home. It caused great difficulties at first, because so many of the wealthy caste Hindus who had supported Gandhi, and hoped he would prove a great national leader, were quite horrified at the idea. But the effect was excellent, for now the men and women who came to join Gandhi knew that they must not only live very simply, but that they must be ready to treat even the humblest and poorest people as brothers and sisters. Not only that, but they must share, as Gandhi did, in the dirtiest jobs. If a young man came to him and talked in fine language about religion or patriotism, saying that he wanted to help in Gandhi's work, then Gandhi would tell him to go and do some unpleasant work that needed to be done. So many were turned away, because that was too hard for them. But those who remained were ready to endure everything gladly; and between such people there was generally good comradeship.

After a year in which he tried to find out all about the problems of his own country, Gandhi made a speech at Benares, the holy city of temples where a Hindu University was being opened. There were many Indian princes at the meeting, which was presided over by an English woman, Mrs. Besant, who was much respected by Indians. Gandhi congratulated the Maharajas on their contributions for the University but suggested that they could do more by leaving their jewels behind! Mrs. Besant was quite horrified and put an end to his speech, but Gandhi went on saying things of that sort and many people felt that here, at last, was a leader who really talked blunt sense and feared nobody, caring only

93

for the truth and for the needs of the country—especially of the poor.

The *ashram* at Sabarmati soon became a great center of activity. It was only a simple collection of low buildings, most of them divided into rooms like the cells of a monastery and bare of furniture. Around it were newly planted trees and farmland, and below, close by the river, a stretch of sand where Gandhi and his friends met before dawn and at sunset for prayers. But the evening prayers soon became an occasion to which thousands might come if something important was happening; for it was then that Gandhi would speak to his followers and to all others who were present.

In 1917 Gandhi was begged to go to a place called Champaran, close to the great Himalaya mountains. Here white settlers had taken possession of much land and forced their Indian tenants to grow indigo for their factories, where a dye was made from the plant. The Indian tenants were little better than slaves, taxed by the landlords—mostly white men —for every conceivable reason. The landlords taxed every home and every marriage and even levied special taxes to pay for their own hunting or holidays. Gandhi went to Champaran to find out about the troubles of the tenants and soon the Government told him he must leave Champaran, but he refused to leave.

He was summoned for disobeying the order and told the court that he had to obey "the higher law of our being, the voice of conscience." The Government suddenly withdrew the case against him and made no further objection to his re-

94

maining in the district. In the end the Government itself was shamed into setting up a committee to inquire into the grievances of the tenants and asking Gandhi to serve on this committee. The result was a victory for the tenants. Some of the money extorted from them had to be returned by the landlords and many abuses were stopped by the Government. India now began to look to Gandhi as a leader—a new kind of leader altogether.

Rising Tide of Patriotism

In his new home, Ahmedabad, Gandhi took up the cause
of the workers in the cotton mills and led them in a successful
strike against the owners—Indians, this time. That struggle
was hardly over when he was asked to help the people of
Kheda—another district in Gujerat—who were pleading in
vain for suspension of taxes during what was nearly a famine
in their part of the country. He led a tax-resistance movement, which was partially successful. British Government

97

officials, some of whom had recently praised him, became very hostile. And then, suddenly, there he was recruiting for the army in the very place—Kheda—where he had recently been preaching non-violent resistance.

Some of his best friends refused, at this point, to work with him. An Indian professor who had been one of his staunchest supporters in Champaran told him bluntly that he couldn't square this recruiting campaign with *ahimsa* (non-violence) and that he felt no loyalty to the British Empire. The people whom Gandhi had so recently led in a struggle against the Government received him very coolly when he returned to preach the virtue of enlistment. "You are a votary of *ahimsa*," they said, "how can you ask us to take up arms?" And again: "What good has the Government done for India to deserve our co-operation?" Gandhi, on the other hand, issued strange leaflets at this time saying that the worst thing the British had ever done in India was to prevent Indians bearing arms. This, he said, was an opportunity for Indians who enlisted to get them back. All this is difficult to understand; but one thing at least was clear and it had great importance later: Gandhi believed that various rather vague statements by British leaders during the First World War meant that India was promised freedom when the war was over or very soon after.

Illness interrupted this recruiting campaign. Gandhi nearly died. By the time he recovered the war was over. And the hope for which he had abandoned "non-violence" turned out to be valueless. So far from being free, India in 1919 appeared to be farther than ever from freedom.

At the end of the First World War the most powerful country in the world was clearly the United States. And the American President talked of "self-determination"—the right of the people in every country to choose how they would be governed.

Indians were delighted, because in their own great country, which seemed to have been asleep so long, people were saying just the same thing. But in New Delhi the British rulers did not seem to have heard of this idea—though so many hints about freedom for India had been made by the Government in London when the war was going badly. Instead of freedom there were new laws which Gandhi and his friends considered outrageous.

They had put up with special laws during the war. As the chief object in wartime is to defeat the enemy, every government at such times makes special laws which dispense with the ordinary safeguards of justice and truth. People can be imprisoned without trial in most countries, during a war; and the right to tell the truth is suspended by censorship of news. Many Indians had objected to such measures in India—though others, including Gandhi, had told them to be patient. But, now that peace had come, new laws, like those introduced during the war, were imposed instead of the self-government for which every self-respecting Indian had hoped.

People were still to be kept in prison without trial. Where trials *did* take place they could be held in secret. In such trials a man accused of some crime could not confront his accusers and, if they were lying, try to prove it by the usual method of cross-examination—indeed, he was not even allowed a lawyer to defend him and did not so much as know the names of those who gave evidence against him; so that even the most innocent person would have had very little chance if enemies had determined to get rid of him. There was, of course, no jury; and there could be no appeal against the secret decisions of these courts.

Far back in the middle ages Englishmen had begun their struggle against this sort of thing in their own country; and educated Indians knew that those who had suffered and fought for fair and open trials by jury were among the real heroes of English history. Almost every section of the Indian population that was organized protested vigorously. Until that time there had been little response, from the great mass of Indians, to the political movements in the country. After the crushing of the Indian "Mutiny" of 1857 they had remained sullen and hopeless, accepting all that happened as "fate." But now there was a popular movement. It was strongest in the Punjab, a northern province which had bred fearless soldiers for centuries.

Gandhi could feel the rising tide of Indian patriotism. He could not stop it and he did not desire to, for he shared in the general resentment against the new laws and the growing desire for freedom. His job, as he saw it, was to accept and welcome the new popular movement, but to do his utmost to keep it peaceful. He was only partly successful. Under great provocation many of the Punjabis took to violence; and when that happens the criminals in any society have their opportunity, just as they do in war. While Hindus and Muslims throughout the rest of India joined in orderly demonstrations and long remained peaceful, even when people were assaulted or fired upon by the police, ugly incidents of cruelty and violence were reported from the Punjab.

Gandhi was not concerned with the question of "who started it." Under the greatest injuries and insults he expected his people to remain peaceful. They could say what they liked about his recruiting for Britain's wars. In the struggle before India, of which he had already become the greatest leader, his terms of enlistment were very different. Early in April, 1919, he hurried north, intending to exert his moral authority on the Punjabis and plead with them to keep the peace at all costs. Instead of allowing him to reach the Punjab, the Government had him arrested on the way and sent back to Bombay.

Other leaders who were trying to keep the people peaceful in the Punjab were deported. Further atrocities were committed on both sides. And then came an event which shocked the whole of India when the story of it at last leaked through the strict censorship of news.

On April 13th, when a peaceful meeting was being held at the town of Amritsar, in a walled public garden, General Dyer, having blocked the only exit with his troops, ordered them to fire and keep on firing into the crowd. For a long time the news of this massacre was kept from the Press and officially nothing was known about it, even in the British Parliament. When, at last, news leaked out, an official inquiry was ordered. It was found that 379 persons had been killed and over 1,100 wounded—these being left unattended. It was also admitted that countless Indians had been publicly and ruthlessly flogged for refusing to grovel to the British and that General Dyer had given an order for Indians to be forced to crawl on their stomachs in a street where one of the mob outrages had been committed (this was an attack on a woman missionary).

Very much more could be said of that reign of terror, which lasted for months, but this may be enough to explain the horror which Gandhi felt. However, when the news of the massacre and of what had followed reached him he was not only horrified at what the Government had done. Outside the Punjab the peaceful demonstrations had broken down with the news of Gandhi's arrest on the way to Amritsar. What was to have been a great campaign against the new laws had begun with what is called a *hartal*—which means that all factories, shops and offices were closed and the economic life of the country was paralyzed. The *hartal*, lasting one day, had been an astonishing success—it was so widely supported and so peacefully carried out. Forms of civil disobedience were to follow—the breaking of certain laws in a carefully planned campaign—and a beginning had been made by the illegal sale of books which the Government had banned. One of these books, oddly enough, was a translation of an English classic, *Unto This Last* by John Ruskin!

But Gandhi's arrest, in spite of his quick release, caused a sudden surge of anger. He saw that, if the movement he had started was indeed to be non-violent, he had started too soon and without sufficient training of his followers. For they *were* his followers, and that was really clear for the first time.

They might be—and indeed they were—an undisciplined mass of people who paid little attention to his words. But he alone had all India looking to him for leadership. Somehow the story of the man who lived humbly and simply and stood up to great men and governments had reached even the people who couldn't read or write. From now on a terrible responsibility lay on him.

In front of him was the challenge of the Amritsar massacre; but before it happened he had already used his great moral authority to stop the campaign which he had done so much to start. He would rather be alone than with an undisciplined rabble behind him. It would take time to train them, beginning with a select few. And meanwhile he had to face this new horror somehow. He was anxious to go himself to the Punjab and investigate—all the more so because some young Punjabis were very angry with him for having stopped the movement of Civil Disobedience. They even said that, if he had not done so, the massacre at Amritsar would never have taken place; and some had gone so far as to threaten his life if he entered the Punjab. So it was like South Africa over again, where he had been between two fires. But the Government still refused, for six months, to let him enter this province and permission was not finally granted until October.

An English friend, Charles Andrews, had arrived before him. Andrews had worked with him earlier on South African and other affairs. No Englishman was ever so deeply loved in India, and of all Gandhi's many English friends he was the closest and the one he most valued. His reports of what had happened were among the first to reach the outside world. Gandhi, when he was at last allowed to visit the Punjab, started a slow, methodical investigation, with some distinguished Indians who had joined him. The Government report, in its stark and frightful facts, was bad enough; but Gandhi's report showed that, even so, there had been a determined effort to shield certain people by concealing or neglecting evidence. And—though he was never interested in revenge or vindictive punishments, he was deeply shocked at the inaction of the Government when its own report was published. General Dyer retired from his command, but the Governor of the Punjab (Sir Michael O'Dwyer), who had approved all the General's actions, was not even reprimanded. Nor was anybody else. To many—perhaps to most—Indians, this seemed "the last straw." Gandhi, who knew the terrible truth, better than anyone, remained remarkably calm. He had hoped that Britain's intentions were good. Evidently, he said, he had been mistaken.

New pressure must be exerted, if only to provide some peaceful outlet for the people, whose feelings had been so much roused by the events since the war. Gandhi returned the medal that had been given him by the Viceroy. The great Indian poet, Rabindranath Tagore, who had never interested himself previously in politics and had accepted a knighthood from the King, repudiated an honor which he could no longer wear with dignity after the Punjab atrocities. Indians everywhere were asked to return and refuse any such honors from the British Government. There was a movement to boycott the courts of law, led by the great Indian lawyer, Motilal Nehru, whose son was one day to be the first Prime Minister of a free India. People were urged to buy no foreign goods, so that British trade with India was severely hit. There was a big effort to persuade Indians not to serve the Government as soldiers, policemen, civil servants or in any other way. By the end of 1920 Gandhi was the undisputed head of the All-India National Congress, which at last really represented the people of India. Its object was Home Rule; its method "non-co-operation"—just not working with the Government—to be followed by the defiance of carefully selected laws when the time seemed to be ripe and the people prepared.

As to the readiness of the people, Gandhi was uncertain. He was known everywhere now as the "Mahatma" (Great Soul) —a title first used by the poet Tagore. Gandhi, who loved Tagore, loathed the title he had bestowed on him and always frowned when people used it. "I am *not* a Mahatma," he would say—sometimes quite irritably. The people shouted "Mahatma Gandhijiki jai" ("Victory to Mahatma Gandhi") but all the same, said Gandhi, no one was willing to listen to him.

His worst fears were realized in February, 1922, at a place called Chauri Chaura. Here some policemen fired on a crowd which was demonstrating against the Government. The crowd turned on the police, who took refuge in the city hall, which was at once surrounded and set in flames. Some of the police died in the fire; others, trying to escape, were cut down by the furious mob outside.

Gandhi had condemned the British Government for taking the Amritsar massacre so lightly. It was now his turn to show what he thought a leader should do when his followers committed wanton murder. Civil Disobedience was about to start within a matter of days, by a refusal to pay taxes in a carefully selected part of the country. Most of the other Indian leaders were already in jail, Gandhi having been left at large, perhaps because of the fear that his arrest would bring about a storm of violence—or perhaps because the Government knew that, if anyone in India could prevent bloodshed, this was the man. The Chauri Chaura murders showed that even Gandhi could not quite do that, though hundreds of millions remained peaceful.

He refused to take the risk of another such incident. The people, he considered, were still not ready for a struggle on his chosen lines. Faced by his refusal to lead, his colleagues had no choice. They agreed to call off the campaign of Civil Disobedience, for there was nobody else who would have had the confidence of India if it had been known that he acted without Gandhi's support. Gandhi himself fasted for five days in penance for the crime committed at Chauri Chaura— which was no doubt what he would have considered the proper behavior of the British Prime Minister when he was told of the atrocities in the Punjab.

Many Indians believed that they had been within reach

of independence. Perhaps they were right. Certainly the Government had been very alarmed; and now, suddenly this unaccountable little man had called off the struggle. He had never been less popular since the days of his unsuccessful compromise with General Smuts in South Africa.

The Government might well have been grateful to an opponent who had shown himself so determined to avoid violence, even though his action had cost him—for the moment—the love and confidence of millions. While Gandhi was a danger they had left him at liberty, though fifty thousand of his supporters had been imprisoned. But now, when he had made himself powerless, they arrested him. He was sentenced to six years in jail.

Fight without Violence

Gandhi remained in prison at Poona until January, 1924, when he had to be hurried to hospital for an operation—he had acute appendicitis. His Indian and British friends were alarmed. So were the rulers of India. If he died people might suspect foul play, regard him as a martyr and (remembering their old leader—but not what he had taught them) start violent demonstrations against the Government. So Gandhi, before the operation, signed a statement to say that he was being well treated and that he had agreed to the operation—also that there must be no demonstration against the Government, whatever happened.

The Government once more had reason to be grateful, for he nearly died; and only a sheet of paper, signed in the presence of well-known Indian witnesses, would have been their safeguard. It may have been partly out of gratitude that he was released when he recovered.

For nearly six years after that Gandhi's work in India was so quiet that his name hardly ever appeared in English newspapers. In prison he had written the story of his life—*My Experiments with Truth*—almost as though he felt that his work was finished. Most British people in India certainly thought so and, by 1929, regarded him as a "spent force." In London a Member of Parliament asked a friend from India, "What has happened to that fellow Gander, or some such name, who used to give us so much trouble?"

The answer was not to be found in the headlines, which so often tell us unimportant things. Really important work, on the other hand, is not always "news." In the villages of India "this fellow Gander" had become a familiar figure. He now wore the simple loin cloth of white hand-spun and hand-woven cotton. In cold weather a cotton shawl covered his shoulders. His head was shaven, making him look bald, and older than he was. He wore spectacles and had no teeth—for, though he had an artificial set, he considered it vanity to wear them except during meals! But he had a wonderful smile which charmed people; and while others called him

"Mahatma," all his friends—who were numbered in thousands—called him simply "Bapu" ("Daddy").

Millions of Indians could not afford to dress better, and he did not wish to be better clothed than they were. This was one of many small things that made him very dear to the poor. For nearly six years he had little to do with politics. He talked to simple people about the problems of their own towns or villages.

In the hot, dry days, before the annual rainy season began, country people could do nothing on the land. But they were mostly very poor, said Gandhi, and yet had to sell part of their crops to buy clothes. Every year food was sent abroad from this starving country so that clothes could be bought—mainly from England. What was the sense in that? Let them keep the food that was so much needed and learn to spin and weave and make clothes for themselves. Thus the idle months could be used profitably. Clever people said it was stupid to revive hand spinning and hand weaving, because there were better and quicker ways of making cloth. But Gandhi didn't look at it that way. How could it be stupid to use time that would otherwise be wasted? The money value of the work done might be very small, but Gandhi knew that it was big enough to make a real difference to people who lived so near to starvation.

This was also a quiet way of putting pressure on the British Government; for the British had gone to India for trade, and trade was still one of their chief interests in the country. But now they had an interesting choice: they could go on ruling

India and lose all their trade, or they could let India be free and hope to regain some trade, later, with a friendly, independent country. And Gandhi himself made it clear that an independent India *would* be friendly to Britain. But the boycott of foreign goods had been criticized by people who said it would help Indian mill owners to make big profits. Hand spinning and hand weaving again seemed to offer an answer. Nobody would make big profits that way: it would only bring a little much needed money to the poor. And how else, in fact, did anybody propose to help them to use those months of idleness in the villages? What they did must be something they could do at home.

Even that was not all. What Gandhi was always looking for was something that every man, woman and child could do. Nobody must feel that he was powerless and that only clever people could serve India. Also, as we have seen, Gandhi liked to teach by example—and here was an excellent opportunity. The spinning wheel he took with him had a very special meaning for him and for all who saw and heard him as he sat, quietly spinning, in a railway carriage or at a conference. On the flag of independent India today there is a wheel; and it would be fair enough to say that it is Gandhi's spinning wheel—the symbol of unity through work.

His speeches and the articles he wrote spoke of many other things which were important to poor and humble people. In South Africa and, since his return, in India too he had worked very closely with Muslims. But there were some Hindus and some Muslims who did not want this unity.

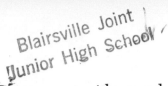

It didn't suit the Government, either; and there were many ways in which it was possible to stir up hatred between people of these two great religions. So all the time Gandhi had to teach Hindu-Muslim unity. It was a campaign that you could begin in your own street and again it would be taught by example. Gandhi was seen all over India with his Muslim friends and fellow workers.

Then there was "Untouchability." This concerned every Hindu. How could they demand rights from the British if they themselves oppressed these downtrodden people who did all the dirty work? We have seen already how Gandhi used example in this work—having "Untouchables" as members of his *ashram* and himself doing the dirty jobs which only "Untouchables" were supposed to do. When he spoke at big meetings, if he saw the "Untouchables" standing apart he would tell the people to mix up. If they refused he would go and stand in the middle of the group of "Untouchables," so that the proud caste Hindus had to crowd in close to hear and so that they could see plainly what their leader thought of these despised people.

In spite of his having been such a little tyrant with his wife, as a boy and as a young man, he had also come to have a great respect for women. Perhaps Kasturbai, by her stubborn independence, had taught him something. He was now opposed to child marriages and to all the restrictions which kept girls uneducated and kept women out of the public life of the country. He believed that most women would understand the principles of *satyagraha* better than

113

most men, because he thought they were naturally more gentle. He was convinced that they had a big part to play in the awakening of India. There were millions of women—especially Muslim women—who rarely left their homes, where they were shut up in a special part of the house. When they did go out, they had to be heavily veiled. In response to Gandhi's appeal for women helpers, thousands broke free from these old restraints.

More and more helpers were needed. The campaign had to be carried into every corner of India. Gandhi's *ashram* was soon the first and principal training center among many such centers, up and down the country, where men and women in their white *khadis* (hand-spun and hand-woven cotton) came and went, learned and taught. People in Britain knew nothing of this. British people in India, if they heard of it, thought that Gandhi was just a crank. At least it was a good thing, they said, that he'd given up leading mass movements and no longer appeared to take much interest in politics. Many Indians, who did *not* think that a good thing, could not see what Gandhi hoped to achieve by it. A few Indians, who had enough money, were now allowed to vote and to send members to a Legislative Assembly at New Delhi—also to Provincial "parliaments." Many of Gandhi's old friends now thought they should try to get elected to these institutions. Gandhi had never been a candidate and he had never even voted; but for a very short time he had taken the same view. Why did he now shake his head?

The truth was that he had no faith now in this way. Because only people with enough money could vote, the land-lords and other people with property stood a much better chance than the poor and these wealthy people were often in league with the Government, because it protected them and they feared big changes in a free India. There were also seats, out of all proportion to their numbers, reserved for the representatives of the Europeans and the Anglo-Indians (people half Indian and half European) and other small communities, most of them favorable to the Government. In the Assembly there were also Government officials and people nominated by the Government. In no circumstances could the All India National Congress possibly have obtained a majority of the seats. The most important subjects were not even entrusted to these "parliaments," but were left to the Viceroy and the Provincial Governors. These high officials could also use their veto to stop any decision of the "parliaments" from becoming law. Or, if they refused to pass any law which the Government wanted, the Viceroy or the Governor in question could just make it law by special powers which allowed him to override them.

Gandhi now believed that only by non-violent struggle could freedom be won—this playing at parliaments he now regarded merely as a means of keeping educated Indians in a perpetual dream. But he had twice failed in his efforts to create a peaceful mass movement, and this time he was de-termined to take his time and do the job thoroughly. He must attack first the evils in the life of his own people, and of these we have seen some examples. This must be done for its own sake and also to create unity and discipline. He wanted a united movement of Hindus and Muslims and "Untouchables," of men and women—why, the emancipation of women alone would double its strength! And in all this work he had a wonderful opportunity to explain his ideas about non-violence. He spoke of this always as a deeply religious man, already revered as a saint in a country where holy men are greatly respected.

As to the nationalist politicians, he could afford to wait for them to come round to his point of view. Once he had been in a hurry. Now he was not. Many of these politicians cared, as he did, about the social evils of India. The British, too, might deplore them—but the Government would never do anything to remove them. Only a free India could finally do that. In New Delhi they were concerned with power, and a foreign government always had quite enough trouble to face without asking for more. The Indian politicians would see—even if they passed good laws which interfered with bad Indian customs the Government would find a way to make them ineffective. In the Indian Army and Police Force the principle of "Untouchability" was carefully observed. You might as well expect the Government to quarrel with the princes and the landlords, who were almost their only friends, as to fall foul of bad old customs, any more than they could help.

It all worked out as he expected. When the nationalists in the Legislative Assembly tried to make child marriages illegal, for example, the Government and its nominated members opposed them. Writers of books and newspaper articles attacking India (and Gandhi) regularly referred to this bad custom; yet, when Indians tried to get rid of it, the Government—which the same writers always praised—did its best to stop reform! In the end, rather than let the world see how things stood, the Government withdrew its opposition. Its members did not vote for the bill, but remained neutral. When the law was passed, however, only the Government could enforce it—and it made no attempt to do so.

Gandhi, working away at the very grass roots of good and evil among the people of India, could afford to smile. Hindu-Muslim unity was still incomplete and unsafe, but "Untouchability" was beginning to crumble. Women were in the forefront of the work. At Bardoli a tax-resistance movement (against overassessment) had been conducted in 1928 and 87,000 peasants had maintained complete self-control through a prolonged struggle, winning the substance of their demand. Gandhi had been saying for years that Swaraj (Self-government) began with one's own self-control, and here was evidence at last of effective training. By the end of the following year the nationalist politicians were ready for a renewal of satyagraha. So, it seemed, was India, And Gandhi was stronger than ever.

He never started such a struggle without first trying to reach an agreement with his opponents. He tried, but without success. The President of the All India National Congress was Jawaharlal Nehru, the future Prime Minister of India, at that time a man of about forty and much admired by the younger and the more progressive Indians. But if there was to be *satyagraha* nobody doubted that it was Gandhi who should lead it. It was also Gandhi's own choice that the first step should be to break the law which made the manufacture of salt a Government monopoly.

Once more the rulers had to consider whether to arrest him—and when, if they did. To arrest him at once would not stop the campaign. Hundreds of thousands were trained and ready. The Government had learned by now that arrests only served to make such a movement more popular. It was no disgrace to go to prison—Gandhi had made people feel that it was the highest honor. And then, if Gandhi and his trained followers were removed, what new and unpleasant form might the mass movement take?

On March 12th, 1930, Gandhi set out from Sabarmati to walk to the sea through hundreds of villages, accompanied by seventy-eight men and women. When they reached the sea they would manufacture salt—illegally—from the sea water. India and half the world watched through the newspapers, the news films and the radio, by which the "salt march" was reported from day to day. All over India people were soon breaking laws and in many places, where the police could not control crowds, it was shown that only the trained and disciplined *satyagrahis* could do so. They were able to do this because they were respected—they were the leaders of the people, by their own choice.

Gandhi was by no means the first of the sixty thousand people arrested that year. The Government surrounded his camp one night with armed police, as though he had been a dangerous outlaw. There was no trial this time—not that it would have mattered. The *satyagrahis* always pleaded guilty in court and did not defend themselves. Prison was even a relief to Gandhi—it was the nearest thing he ever had to a holiday, for he did the work of three or four people. (He could only deal with letters and other writing jobs now by having a "Silence Day" once a week!) In prison, too, he worked, rising for prayers at four o'clock every morning, spinning, reading and writing; but there were not so many interruptions and he was, at such times, free of his many responsibilities. When the poet Tagore had once said that he envied Gandhi's health, Gandhi had laughed and said: "If you behaved yourself you would get an arrest cure." He had many of these "cures" in his life.

The struggle that followed was conducted peacefully by the people in most parts of the country. There were, of course, some exceptions. Not all the people were prepared to follow Gandhi's methods and some even belonged to secret underground organizations (like the French Resistance Movement under the German occupation, a few years later). But many foreign journalists and visitors were amazed to see how peaceful the Indian crowds remained even when the police charged them with their *lathis* (sticks) and even when armed police or soldiers fired at them. Even worse things happened, though nothing quite as bad as the Amritsar massacre or the cruelties which followed.

By 1931, it was clear that the Government would have to give way sooner or later. British trade with India was

119

practically ruined. There were signs that Indian soldiers could no longer be relied on when used against their unarmed and defenseless countrymen—not even when the soldiers belonged to one religion and the people to another. Then an astonishing thing happened. Gandhi made a "pact" with the Viceroy and persuaded most of the other Congress leaders to agree to it.

Explaining Gandhi was always difficult. Gandhi made this pact in order to talk things over in London at what was called the "Round Table Conference" where Indians were discussing the future of India with representatives of the British Government. A year before, Gandhi had refused to go to this conference. What made him change his mind was never clear. He was a bit of a puzzle to everybody, as usual.

Before the "pact" was made, which meant that Civil Disobedience was ended and the *satyagrahi* prisoners released by the Government, Gandhi tried to persuade the Viceroy to have an inquiry into the behavior of his police, who had been widely accused of using torture. But this was refused, as the Viceroy did not want to discourage the police, because he said they might be wanted for the same work again. This refusal made it harder than ever to get other leaders to agree to the "pact"; but somehow Gandhi had his way.

The elder Nehru had recently died. His son, who was already, probably, second only to Gandhi in popularity, was among those who strongly opposed the "pact." But the opinion of the other leaders did not matter with the mass of Indians. Their Mahatma was, it seemed, above criticism; and he was received everywhere with wild enthusiasm. At the end of August, 1931, he left for London.

From Palace to Prison

It was forty-four years since the shy young Mohandas had first arrived in England, hopelessly embarrassed because of his white suit. The man who now arrived was also dressed in white, and much more oddly—but he was not in the least embarrassed. He came, in spite of the English winter that lay before him, in the same scanty clothes that he would have worn in India, and in these clothes he bore the bitter weather.

He was perfectly at ease. At the very moment of his arrival, with "important" people there to meet him on the quay, he kept them waiting while he greeted trusted personal friends in his cabin. He stayed in the East End of London, becoming a familiar sight to the workers and housewives and small shopkeepers in the neighborhood.

Once, in India, when a doctor had treated Gandhi free, the great leader had asked him if he would also treat his 400,000,000 countrymen without charge. The doctor had replied that Gandhi represented the people, so he *was* serving four hundred million Indians! "You're talking like a fourth-class lawyer," Gandhi had replied. But there was much truth in the doctor's words. And yet here his voice at the Round Table Conference was just one among many—Indian princes, for example. Most of them were soon to be swept away, but a great deal of fuss was made of them in London at the time. And the smallest minorities, such as the white people living in India, had their representatives. In the Conference Gandhi's voice seemed almost lost among so many. There were special "representatives" for the Muslims, but only for those Muslims who were against him—and Gandhi in vain reminded people that millions of Muslims supported him and supported the Congress.

But though the Conference did not seem to be of much value, some good came of Gandhi's visit to England, because British people at last met him and saw that he was not a bogey-man or just a joke but somebody that they had to respect—even to love. The Government, for example, appointed two detectives to go with him everywhere. He was used to being followed about by detectives, but these men were not there to spy on him. They were for his protection. He did not want to be protected, but he was a guest in England and accepted the arrangement, which was kindly intended. He worked such long hours that the detectives had a hard time—beginning every morning before dawn, when Gandhi (after prayers) would take a walk. And he walked so fast that these big, burly policemen almost had to run to keep up with him! But they came to love him and when he went back to India one of them said that he felt like a mother who had lost her child.

Before Gandhi returned, trouble had begun in India. The Government had started arresting patriots again, including Gandhi's good Muslim friends, the Pathans of the Northwest Frontier, and the popular leader, Jawaharlal Nehru. As before, the toy parliaments had been ignored and the Government was using special powers of the same kind which had begun all the trouble in 1919—imprisoning without trial, suppressing newspapers and so on.

On his return, Gandhi decided to start Civil Disobedience again and was soon back in prison at Poona. While he was in jail the British Government was planning a new constitution for India. It was not so bad as the old one, though it did not begin to look like real freedom; but the thing which upset Gandhi most was the arrangement for representing a small proportion of the "Untouchables" in the new "parliaments."

Till that time the "Untouchables" had not had any votes. The Government had appointed people who were supposed to represent them, including a man called Dr. Ambedkar. Everybody in India knew that the best friend the "Untouchables" had was Gandhi himself. He had suffered much in his defense of them and in his determined efforts to secure their rights. Dr. Ambedkar's idea of helping the "Untouchables" was to attack Gandhi continually, and everything he said or did. Naturally Gandhi wanted the "Untouchables" (the *Harijans* as he called them, meaning "Children of God") to have the vote. It was their right and would enable them to choose real representatives, instead of the Government appointing men like Ambedkar; for such people went about giving a false impression outside India by calling themselves "leaders of the Depressed Classes."

But Gandhi wanted to abolish "Untouchability" altogether. He did not want to have these wretched people regarded as a class forever separate. Considering their numbers, the number of representatives they were to have was ridiculously low, as he pointed out. What he wanted was the full rights of citizenship for all, including all *Harijans;* but the Government proposals separated them from the caste Hindus. Gandhi had often fasted by way of penance or protest; and in 1932 he began a long fast in protest against this betrayal of the *Harijans,* as he considered it. The whole of India was shocked and there were hasty consultations. As usual, there was a compromise, to which Gandhi and the British Government agreed. By this compromise the representation of the *Harijans* was more than doubled, though it did not entirely remove the principle of "separation" to which Gandhi had objected.

He said of the new constitution, as a whole: "You tell me that I am to be master in my own house. But you keep the key of the safe and you station a sentry at the door." When this constitution came into operation he was free again; but—as before—he was not a candidate for any election. He has often been called a politician, but he never once took part in politics, as most people use the word. To the very end his authority, which was enormous, was only the moral authority of a man who was loved and almost worshipped by the vast majority of his countrymen.

The All India National Congress meanwhile decided to contest the elections under the new constitution. Though everything was weighted against them by over-representation of minorities and by the exclusion of most poor people from the vote, the Congress scored a startling victory. But two years later the world was at war again; and in this emergency—as Gandhi and Nehru had both seen from the beginning—the new constitution was shown to be a mere shadow. India was at war because Britain was at war; and Indian votes in Assembly or Council would make no difference to what happened. The game of politics was suddenly over, and all that remained was a mass movement, many trained leaders in towns and villages, and an old man of seventy who—in prison or out of it—had more power than any king on earth.

The Price of Victory

In spite of his popularity Gandhi was beginning to feel lonely. Some Indians were in favor of helping Britain in the war—as he himself had been, on earlier occasions—without conditions. Others would have helped if they could have been sure, from the behavior and promises of the Government, that they would have been fighting for freedom. Some, made bitter and reckless by the long struggle, were even prepared to work with the enemies of Britain, hoping that their victory would at last bring freedom to India.

Gandhi and a few faithful followers rejected all these ways. He said this time that he stood for "out-and-out non-violence" and could not barter it, even for the freedom of India. He also said that he knew, this time, that he did not speak for the people. When Japan came into the war and it looked as though India might be invaded he said that complete non-co-operation and *satyagraha* methods should be used against them. At the same time he was at first against any campaign of mass civil disobedience against the British during the war, for various reasons. There was so much division of opinion, so much violent feeling; and it was too easy for such a movement to become—or at least to appear—a means of helping the Germans and the Japanese. He objected to British rule, thought Japanese rule would be worse, and objected to fighting for or against either—or even for the freedom that he so passionately wanted.

Back in 1929 he had said about his friends of the All India National Congress: "Congress used me as their tool, and I am a willing tool. But the day will come when I shall say 'No' and our ways will part." That day had now come. Much as they loved Gandhi, the Congress leaders were ready to give up "non-violence." They wanted a deal with the Government. They would fight now, if there was to be something worth fighting for.

And now Gandhi, who had been known for so long as a man who led a life of self-sacrifice but was always happy and full of laughter, became very sad. But he was bound up now with his people and with the whole world. "A person who believes in non-violence," he had said, "believes in a living God. He cannot accept defeat."

In 1942 his old opponent, Winston Churchill (who had even refused to meet him, ten years before, when Gandhi was in London) suddenly made very much better offers to India than any British Prime Minister had ever made before. It meant much greater freedom than India had ever known, under British rule, with complete freedom—if India wanted it—promised after the war. It was a compromise which would have been accepted in 1932—but now it was rejected. It was rejected by Congress, because the Congress leaders knew now that they were going to win in this long struggle. They would no longer accept compromises or trust promises, remembering what had happened in 1919.

It was clear that the British Government was not going to trust the people of India with much real power at once—so Indians felt *they* could not trust the British to hand it over after the war. For a little while Gandhi and his old friends in the Congress could work together once more. Mass Civil Disobedience was to begin again; but before it began Gandhi was arrested, with many other leaders.

He had avoided calling for mass civil disobedience as long as he felt he could do so. The spirit of violence which the war had let loose had affected India deeply, and there were soon outbreaks of violence all over the country. This time Gandhi was a prisoner in a palace. As usual, there had not been any trial, but in this last imprisonment he was treated rather like a specially honored prisoner of war. From his palace prison he protested against Government statements which accused him and his Congress friends of having organized this violence. In other occupied countries this kind of resistance was common enough and was considered quite right; but he did not believe in it and knew that it was no part of the Congress plan, either.

Kasturbai shared this "imprisonment" with her husband. In the intimate circles where he had so long been known as "Daddy" she had been the Mother. She had proved equal to the responsibilities thrust upon her as the wife of Gandhi and was dear to the whole country, as a fearless worker who had helped to rouse the women of India. In 1944 she died in the palace at Poona, deeply lamented by the whole country for her own sake and because people shared in Gandhi's grief. Kasturbai had been the first to share in his many adventures. So many others had died. He was nearly seventy-five himself and it looked, for a moment, as though he, too, would die in the palace. He became so ill that the Government decided to release him.

New trouble awaited him on his recovery. All his life he had worked for unity between Hindus and Muslims. So often he had succeeded and for years it had seemed that Congress really was bringing the people of these two great religions together for a common purpose. There had been, for some time, separate Muslim parties which did not want to work with Hindus (though they, too, always said that they wanted freedom). But these parties had not been very successful. The best known of them, the Muslim League, had received a crushing defeat by the Muslim voters in the elections of 1937. But during the war the Muslim League had been growing steadily; and now it demanded a separate, independent state for the Muslims. As Muslims were scattered all over India the only place where this new state could be created was in parts of the north, where they were in the majority. They would call this state "Pakistan," they said.

Gandhi knew this would mean bloodshed. It meant separating the people, making them feel that they were enemies. If there was to be this new state of Pakistan there would still be millions of Muslims in the rest of India and Hindus in Pakistan. With religious feelings roused, what would happen to these people? Would they be safe? He doubted it. But the leader of the Muslim League was a very ambitious man. If Pakistan came into existence, he would be the head of the new state. Any price seemed worth paying for that.

With the end of the war it was clear that independence was very near. Though there was a different government in Britain, the reasons which had influenced Churchill when he made his offer had been strengthened by new events. For various reasons there was much less to be gained by trying to hold India, and clearly it was going to be very difficult. Most Indians had disapproved of the Japanese because of their conquests; but many Indian soldiers, when captured by the Japanese, had gone over to their side. As they were not fighting for a free country, it made little difference to them which side they served. Most Indians were still not sympathetic to the Japanese, but they understood the attitude of the soldiers and there was a tremendous protest when these men were captured and threatened with punishment.

Russia, it was now realized, might easily succeed where Japan had failed. Communist propaganda in such a poor country as India, under foreign rule, might be more effective than an invasion. It was time that the Indians were given something worth defending. Behind the scenes the powerful American Government, for more than one reason, urged that this should be done quickly. A mutiny in the Indian Navy showed that there was no time to lose.

There were, no doubt, many other reasons for the decision to grant freedom to India; but among them all there was, surely, the fact that Gandhi was now respected all over the world. You could put a man like that in prison quite easily, but you felt ashamed of yourself. All the world knew, now, that the prisoner was a much greater man than those who put him in prison. In Britain, too, sympathy for him and his cause had grown steadily, in spite of all the ridicule that had been heaped on this curious man and the lies that had been told about him, which would fill hundreds of books!

There was so much to do; Gandhi had often said that he intended to live to be 125, so that he could have more time to do it! But now that freedom was coming it meant that India was to be divided. This new state of Pakistan was to be carved out of the northern provinces, and all his time and energy would be needed trying to prevent bloodshed. He had sought freedom through non-violence and unity—and now freedom was coming, with disunity and hatred. Even the new, independent India was not going to be built to the pattern he had hoped for. He never wanted an imitation of a Western state, but little men with legal minds were already planning to make it so. In his palace prison someone had read Bernard Shaw's play, *St. Joan,* to Gandhi; and he had laughed at the end, where St. Joan offers to come back to life, but the people who praise her do not want her any more. He was not yet dead, but he felt himself unwanted by the people who praised him.

"Don't you see the loneliness of it all?" It was 1947 and he spoke to a friend, as he walked barefoot on a pilgrimage of penance through villages where there had been rioting. It had started now—the murder of Hindus by Muslims, of Muslims by Hindus. All over India people were celebrating the coming of freedom and shouting *"Mahatma Gandhijiki Jai!"* Gandhi was *not* celebrating; and these cries of "Victory to Mahatma Gandhi" were meaningless. He had lost all interest in living to be 125. Indeed, he felt that death was very near. He could check this violence; and he did, by his appearance in the most dangerous places. He could still calm mobs; and he did, by a barefoot pilgrimage through troubled areas, by fasting, by appearing publicly with a Muslim leader and facing a rioting crowd. But there were Hindus who were bitter against him now, just because he wanted peace with the Muslims. He received many abusive and threatening letters. Stones were thrown at a house where he was staying. It is true that he calmed the mob when he appeared at one

of the broken windows and spoke to them. But he knew that there was worse than mob violence now to face. There were plots against his life.

Eighteen years ago, when an attempt had been made by terrorists to kill the Viceroy he had, of course, publicly deplored such an action. But he had said, in private, "I shall be the next one." It had seemed absurd to others, at the time, but now everybody knew the danger in which he stood. Lord Mountbatten, the last British Viceroy, specially chosen to make a graceful surrender of power into Indian hands, was worried about Gandhi's safety. So were the new Indian Cabinet Ministers. They took precautions. He did not want protection but could not prevent them. But on one thing he managed to have his way. At his meetings for prayer everybody had always been free to come. Here, at least, there should be no question of police protection. When he had withstood the angry crowds in Calcutta and wandered alone through the villages of Bengal Lord Mountbatten had called him his "one-man boundary force." No police had protected him when he stayed in the huts of the poor, so recently. And if protection must now be forced upon him, at least the prayer time must remain as it had always been. Reluctantly his old friends of the new Government agreed.

Gandhi was equally at home with the rich and the poor, though he often boasted that he was a very expensive guest to the rich, for he attacked their consciences and made them give large sums of money to the good causes for which he worked. In Delhi he stayed, in January, 1948, with a wealthy

136

Indian manufacturer, as his usual home when in Delhi, with some *Harijans,* was full of refugees. His message of courage and of repentance had done much to calm the fears and touch the hearts of his people. Even in these troubled times he had impressed the Mountbattens by his warmth and charm and—as Mountbatten noted—"his unfailing sense of humor." In Calcutta he had achieved what seemed a miracle. "The old man has done it again," one astonished observer had said, as he saw Hindus and Muslims celebrating together.

But the ugly murmurs persisted. Some Hindus said openly: "Why didn't the old man die on the day of independence?" As a penance for the evil spirit which he still felt in his country he fasted, for the last time. He was 78. The fast lasted for six days, and, for the first time, there were cries of "let Gandhi die" from some angry Hindus standing outside the house at night. Two days after the fast ended a bomb was thrown by a young Hindu, with the intention of killing him. No one was hurt, but Gandhi alone was untroubled. As before, after the murderous attacks made on him in the past (by white men and by Indians in South Africa) his chief concern was that no action should be taken against the misguided youth who had sought his death.

Had the time come at last when he really *could* return to his work in the villages? It was certainly in his mind. The advice of Dr. Mehta, years ago, on his first visit to London, had made a deep impression on him. It is in the family life of people that we understand them and their needs. He had told it to Christian missionaries and to his own disciples and followed the principle himself. The next struggle, like the last, would be won in the villages—the struggle against poverty, ignorance and disease. Recently he had often been worried as to what he should do. Now he knew once more. He would like to start again, very humbly.

That was his hope. But did he believe it would really be possible? Something in him gave warning that it was not. On the morning of January 30th he dealt with important letters, saying that he must reply to them that day—the next day he might be dead.

That evening, as he came to the place of prayer, a young Hindu named Godse suddenly approached him. Before anyone realized that he had a revolver in his hand, there was a shot, followed by two more. With the first shot Gandhi called twice on the name of God. They were his last words.

Many strange things happened after that. Millions of Muslims knew that Gandhi had died because he was a Hindu who had loved the Muslims and wanted peace with them. Millions of Hindus knew that he, who had struggled against the British and been threatened often by Muslims, had been killed by one of their own number, so that theirs was the everlasting shame. In London the Indian High Commissioner told a meeting of Indians that all of them who had harbored violent thoughts had helped to murder Gandhi. He did even more by his death than he had done while living to bring about a spirit of repentance among his countrymen.

No less strange were the military honors with which the

body of Mohandas Karamchand Gandhi was taken to its cremation. But one thing, at least, would have touched his heart. He had spent many years struggling against the British, while claiming to be their "lifelong and wholly disinterested friend." At last, it seemed, they knew it. Warm words of tribute came from England; and in India the Mountbattens mourned his death as a deep and personal loss.

Another strange thing was that India so soon trampled upon the wishes of Gandhi, throughout his long life, about people who injured him. Nobody can doubt what his last wish would have been, had he been able to speak a few words before he died. He would have asked them to have mercy on the misguided Godse. Knowing this, they hanged Godse and went on worshipping Gandhi in the way which he had always hated.

He had said once: "I have no strength save what God gives me. I have no authority over my countrymen save the purely moral." He well knew how weak that authority often became. Its partial failure, after his death, would have surprised him less than its partial success, for in these and other events we can see both.

The United Nations flag was flown at half-mast when the news reached them, to show that the whole world mourned for a man who was never the head of a state or even a member of any Government, but a private citizen who had died for what he called "the hope of the aching, storm-tossed and hungry world." And that hope was Peace.

Index of Place Names

Africa, 13, 32
Africa, South, 51, 52, 55, 58, 60, 63, 65, 66, 67, 69, 70, 71, 74, 75, 76, 77, 80, 83, 85, 87, 91, 103, 107, 112, 137
African coast, South, 53
African colony, South, 67
African territories, South 83
African Union, South 86
Afrikaner Republic, 75
Ahmedabad, 92, 97
America, 32
Amritsar, 101, 102, 103, 106, 119
Asia, 75
Benares, 93
Bengal, 136
Bhavnagar, 51
Bombay, 15, 30, 31, 32, 33, 34, 43, 45, 47, 53, 70, 71, 75, 91, 92, 101
Bond Street, 37
Britain, 43, 89, 91, 101, 104, 112, 114, 127, 129, 133, 134
British Empire, 98
Calcutta, 69, 136, 137
Cape Colony, 83
Champaran, 94, 98
Chauri Chaura, 105, 106
Charlestown, 57
East, the, 18
Eastern countries, 29
England, 16, 28, 29, 30, 31, 32, 34, 35, 38, 41, 43, 46, 47, 48, 49, 52, 55, 70, 89, 91, 111, 123, 124, 125, 139
Europe, 16, 46, 89
Gujerat, 92, 97
Delhi, 136, 137
Denmark, 15
Durban, 53, 55, 56, 64, 65, 71, 75, 77

Himalaya Mountains, 94
India, 14, 15, 16, 20, 22, 23, 31, 32, 38, 42, 43, 51, 53, 55, 64, 65, 66, 67, 71, 73, 74, 75, 81, 90, 91, 95, 98, 99, 101, 103, 104, 105, 106, 109, 110, 111, 112, 113, 114, 115, 116, 117, 118, 119, 120, 123, 124, 125, 126, 127, 130, 131, 132, 133, 134, 135, 139
Indian Ocean, 53
Ireland, 16
Japan, 130, 134
Johannesburg, 57, 58, 76, 77, 78, 82, 84
Kathiawar, 15, 20, 30, 35, 42, 43, 47, 49, 50, 51, 53, 57, 70, 92
Kensington, 36, 38
Kheda, 97, 98
London, 29, 35, 36, 38, 39, 42, 43, 44, 45, 47, 48, 61, 80, 83, 87, 89, 91, 99, 110, 120, 121, 124, 131, 137, 138
Maritzburg, 57
Natal, 51, 53, 59, 60, 64, 65, 66, 70, 71, 74, 75, 77, 78, 82, 83, 84, 85, 86, 92
New Delhi, 99, 114, 116
Newcastle, 85
Northwest Frontier, 125
Orange Free State, 74, 83
Pakistan, 133, 134
Paris, 44
Phoenix Settlement, 77, 84, 92
Poona, 109, 125, 132
Porbandar, 13, 14, 15, 16, 17, 18, 19, 28, 29, 48, 49, 51, 52, 55, 63
Pretoria, 56, 58, 60, 62
Punjab, 100, 101, 102, 103, 104, 105, 106

Rajkot, 15, 17, 18, 19, 29,
  32, 43, 44, 45, 47, 49,
  50, 52, 60, 67, 69, 70
Richmond, 36
Russia, 134
Sabarmati, River, 92, 94,
  118
Saurashtra, 15
South Africa, 51, 52, 55,
  58, 60, 63, 65, 66, 67,
  69, 70, 71, 74, 75, 76, 77,
  80, 83, 85, 87, 91, 103,
  107, 112, 137

South African coast, 53
South African colony, 67
South African territories,
  83
Southampton, 34, 35
Tolstoy Farm, 84, 92
Transvaal, 59, 61, 62, 64,
  65, 74, 75, 76, 77, 79,
  80, 82, 83, 84, 86, 92
United States, 99
"White City"
  (Porbandar), 15, 17, 29,
  49

Credits

Designer/BERT RAY STUDIO

Illustrations by/PARVIZ SADIGHIAN

Cover Painting/MARY GEHR

Type/CALEDONIA

Paper/ 70# PUBLISHERS OFFSET

Printer/REGENSTEINER CORPORATION

141

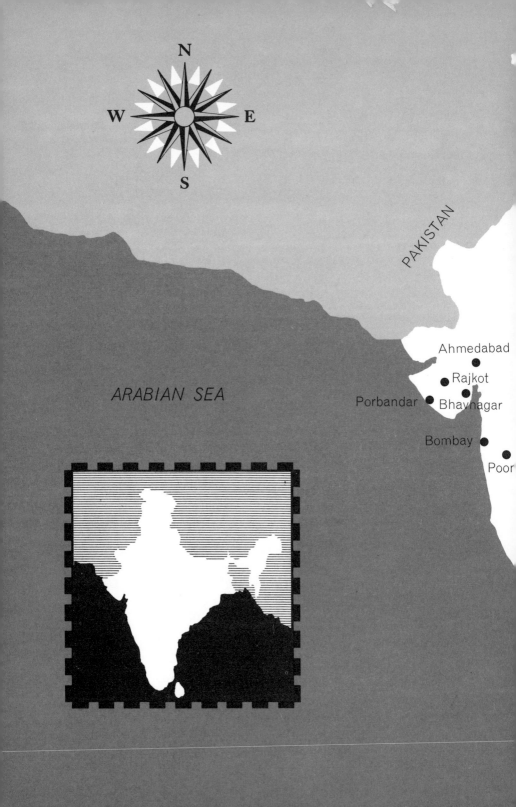

N

W   E

S

PAKISTAN

Ahmedabad

Rajkot

Porbandar Bhavnagar

ARABIAN SEA

Bombay

Poor

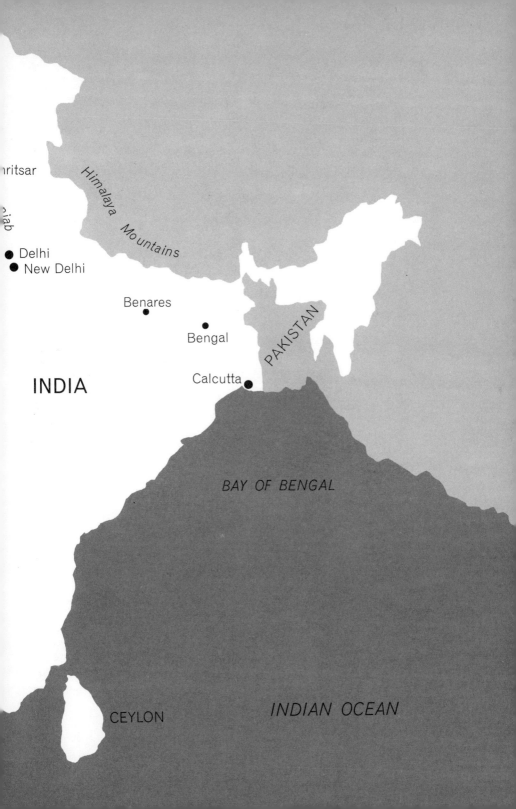

Blairsville Joint
Junior High School

Blairsville Joint
Junior High School

Blairsville Joint
Junior High School

Blairsville Joint
Junior High School

Blairsville Joint
Junior High School

Blairsville Joint
Junior High School

Junior High School